MY LOG

By

E. F. "PAT" SHEERAN

Wingspan Press

Published in the United States and the United Kingdom by WingSpan Press, Livermore, CA

The WingSpan name, logo and colophon are the trademarks of WingSpan Publishing.

ISBN 978-1-63683-003-2 (hardcover)
ISBN 978-1-63683-997-4 (ebk.)

First edition 2021

Printed in the United States of America

www.wingspanpress.com

1 2 3 4 5 6 7 8 9 10

Introduction

Edward Francis Sheeran is my dad; everyone called him Pat. It's an Irish thing. Everyone's called "Pat!" Dad was third-generation Irish, and a family joke is that his older brother's name is Donald but everyone called *him* Pat, Dad's name was Edward but everyone called *him* Pat (except his immediate family), and my brother's name is Patrick, but everyone calls him Duffy.

Dad's dad, Edward Patrick Sheeran, was second-generation Irish, went to school through the eighth grade, and then went to work. From a first job digging ditches to selling shovels, to selling electrical equipment, to starting a store where he sold refrigerators to becoming General Manager of Frigidaire in Dayton, Ohio – his climb upward was remarkable and not impossible in his day.

You might imagine that Edward Patrick was a typical salesman, loud and brash, but my grandfather was neither. He was gentle, had a wry humor and a quiet manner. (His brother, John, did not, although I only heard him spouting against FDR.) I met my grandfather twice: once when we visited Dayton, Ohio – I was five when I met him, six when he visited our house in New Jersey, and he passed away soon after, partly, I suspect, because he missed his wife, who had passed away a few years before. Sheeran men love their wives with an al-most mythical passion.

But I've heard stories about my grandfather that contradict some of that quiet manner. He was a demon on the road, never liking any-one to pass him and revving up to over seventy miles an hour. He introduced us to very hot sauce over shrimp cocktail, and we had shrimp with (very) hot sauce on Christmas Eve, a tradition that has been preserved.

Although I didn't know him well, I'm told he was quite a fellow. He married the elegant Mary Elizabeth McDonald of Dayton. The family joke (yes, another one; there are plenty – for another time) was that while he was on the road selling, she would buy a house and he'd come home to find out he'd moved. That tradition stuck with their daughter Lillian, who would buy a house, fix it up, and then move again.

All three of Edward Patrick's and Mary's children – Don, Mary, and Eddie – went to college and emerged with sparkling personalities. Although separated by distance, the Irish side of the family has remained close. Even now, the next generation can get together – sometimes for sad occasions, sometimes for Zoom pandemic gatherings – and pick right up from where we left off.

My parents had a good marriage. Dad was romantic, funny, affectionate, old fashioned, courtly. Once, when we were having after-church breakfast at a restaurant in town, a man came in swearing at the top of his voice. I was about six years old; I just heard him yelling without understanding, so I'm telling this story as I've heard it. But I do remember Dad getting up, going over to this loudmouth and saying, quietly, "Would you mind keeping your voice down. My wife and children are here." The guy shut up immediately. He also paid for our breakfast. (When I told this story to friends, someone pointed out, "Yeah, but your dad was one big fellow.")

I'm thinking Dad was a lot like his dad.

He loved playing with us kids. He was a hard working manager of a Coca-Cola Bottling plant in Washington, New Jersey for years, and every merchant in town knew and respected him. He sang in the church choir with a natural bass/baritone that melted women in the pews. He livened up parties by imitating a trombone (I've never known anyone else who could do that). He was an officer of the Lion's Club, a member of the town council, he coached the church basketball team, and I swear that our dachshund/terrier was in love with him. Sometimes he sat down with me at the piano and played a song by ear and he'd sing to me – he never had a music lesson -- he played whiffle ball on summer nights with the neighborhood kids, he used to take me around town when he made courtesy (not sales) calls with customers – everyone enjoyed his easygoing humor -- which is why he won so many awards from Coca-Cola.

He was one of the sons-in-law who entered Peg's father, Frank Vlossak's, Coke business, in the days when Coke symbolized "America." Despite the discomfort that frequently accompanies a family business, Dad managed the business better than Frank's sons. Pat didn't like the family business conflicts, and he was always trying to bring people together. His attempts usually ended up in fun, like the rival softball games between the Coke plants in our franchise that he set up over the summer. He was a hard worker, and I remember summer holidays – Memorial Day, Fourth of July – when he had to work all day, so that we had our family barbecues after the holiday. Sometimes, work could pile on so that we often didn't know, until the day, if we would be able to go on our planned summer vacations. We always did, but there was always a little suspense.

He and our mother, Peg, had a circle of friends that were close for decades and held parties that always ended in singing (they dubbed themselves the Sipping and Singing Society). Dad and Mom took us out to dinner once a month (as Peg said, so we would learn how to behave in public). Pat and Peg frequently went on dates, too, and we kids would often find them kissing in the kitchen and dancing in the living room. They never stopped being in love. It was a good feeling.

Edward Francis "Pat" Sheeran was a typical representative of the Greatest Generation. He believed in his family and his country, in decency and honesty, and in hard work; he had frustrations, he wanted to write more than he did, stories and poems – but he entertained the Optimist Club with his humorous and accurate minutes that everyone in town wanted to read. He wrote poems at the drop of a hat – if a fireman died in the line of duty, Dad would rush off a poem in his honor, send it to the widow, and it would be read at the funeral. Sometimes he wrote poems about love of country. When Findlay, Ohio (where my parents moved to in their later years) was declared Flag City, USA, it was because my father started the ball rolling. He was sentimental. When he won a beautiful RCA phonograph, he brought home Mantovani records. When I was six, Walt Disney's *Sleeping Beauty* was coming to our local theater, and he brought me home an abridged version of the ballet score, which had a tremendous influence on me as later years would tell.

The Peg and Pat romance, and you'll read how it started, lasted throughout their entire marriage. When I went to Saint Mary's College where Peg went, the first thing I did was walk their "romance road" – to the Notre Dame grotto, to the log chapel, and even past the cemetery where they had their first kiss – a fact that once caused me giggles, but it's really a lovely spot. And yet, they hardly knew each other – not even two months – before Dad went off to war. Most of their romance occurred in letters. And when Dad came home, item number one was "marry Peg." When you think of the chances – both of them really lucked out.

Like others of his generation who served his country, Dad rarely talked about his service in the war, aside from this book, *My Log*, which he assembled after he was stationed in Boston – probably with the help of the letters he'd written home – and he had copies of the book bound for us and for his parents and brother and sister. As a kid, I read the beginning and end – how he met and married my mother – and skipped over the battles. Putting this together, and finally reading those neglected middle chapters, I found that he really was in the thick of things at Leyte, the kamikazes missing him and his shipmates by mere yards. Reading my father's personal account of WW2 is to understand the sacrifices of that generation. A young man took for granted that he should defend his country. Beneath the lines, you will sense his values and passions, his humor, underlying fears, and his cherishing of home, family, country, and faith as a legacy one would not want to betray. If that sounds dull, you'll notice how often he and his shipmates sought out fun when they could. He might be frustrated that FDR won a fourth term, but he steered that LCI to the beach and manned the guns. He swore to protect the Constitution and the United States from all enemies, foreign and domestic. He met that promise in battle and in life. That some in this country, even those who have taken such an oath, have forgotten what that means would have broken his heart.

My Log was written in 1946; Dad uses a words and has attitudes typical of his place in society at that time. The enemies are the "Japs," but you will notice his compassion for those affected by the war and references to his religious faith. From his father, he inherited a liking for people, and from his mother he won a love of family and keeping holidays: this man owned Christmas in our house. From the Irish, he inherited music, laughter, and a crazy habit of going out into the weather's biggest storms. Well, maybe he got that from the Navy, but I got that from him.

The next voice you hear will be that of Edward Francis Sheeran (with a few asides from me). But you can call him "Pat."

– Mary P. Sheeran (Yup, the "P" stands for Patricia.)

Chapter One

ENLISTMENT

Pearl Harbor meant nothing to me. I didn't even know where it was. The beginning of the war and early in 1942 did not see me realize the full significance of the grave situation that had placed this country in the peril it now found itself. However, little by little, I began to understand that I was also an American citizen and, like the rest of the men my age, due for service. On Valentine's Day of 1942, I registered for the draft but found my name near the bottom of the list on becoming a new soldier. At this time, I was finishing my sophomore year at Xavier University in Cincinnati, and I developed a false sense of security because of my college training. This was soon blasted when some of my friends were drafted almost immediately.

As time went slowly on, I began to give more thought to my part in the war and when I might be pulled into service. I did not give much thought to the branch of service that I preferred, but I was leaning toward the Navy for the reason that I had sailed from New Orleans to Tela, Honduras, and had loved it.

One day, as my memory recalls, it was early May, my father brought home a pamphlet on the newly introduced Navy V-7 program and was somewhat excited about the contents. After reading the pamphlet, I became very interested. In it were stated the following offers: First, upon signing in the V-7 program, the applicant would be placed on inactive duty in the Navy and be allowed to finish college; second, upon graduation, the applicant would then be sent to a Naval Training School for appointment as an Ensign in the United States Navy. At the same time, he must remain single until graduation from Midshipman School. On that point, I was secure.

By June 1, I had stored up enough ambition to job down to the

Naval Recruiting Station in Cincinnati to see what the complete picture was on the subject. I found it to my liking indeed, for no other branch of the service offered anything to compare with it. I signed up and waited my turn for the physical examination. I was nearly finished with that when the Pharmacist Mate on duty discovered, through a slip of my lip, that I had had rheumatism or a reasonable facsimile, and I was out. It was a little stunning, for my crescendo of interest had been mounting all the time, and when I was finally let down, it was a trifle hard.

I went home and waited for my draft call. Another month passed by, and when nothing happened, I tried the Navy again. Relieved to find that my records had been lost, I tried the physical all over again, but to my surprise, I failed. This time, it was because of my eyes. I had just missed. But I was told that I could try again on my eyes, and I did. Time after time, I reported to the station for the eye examination, and each time, I barely missed. The requirements were 20/20 vision in one eye and 18/20 in the other. I had 20/20 vision in the right eye, but only 17/20 in my left. And they wouldn't consider me. Home again, I was placed on a carrot juice and leafy diet to aid me in "regaining" my sight.

The family moved to Dayton in August and, according to the Navy, I had to change my major in school to meet the new requirements for the V-7 program. I chose business and registered at the University of Dayton in the Business Department.

In mid-September, I finally made the eye examination after taking the entire physical over again. It was my seventh try.

However, good fortune was and was not with me in the next two weeks. Driving home from Cincinnati in the middle of the night, I was involved in a terrific automobile wreck when a farmer in Lebanon, Ohio, came out of a side road with no brakes and hit me broadside. To this day, I do not remember passing through Lebanon, and the accident happened three miles beyond the city. My car was hurtled through a fence, played tag with a telephone pole, hit a tree, and buried itself in the mud fifty feet from the road. I was unconscious from the start, I never knew what had hit me. The car was a total wreck, and when I awoke on the operating table, I felt likewise.

I was not operated on, for, by some miracle, it wasn't needed. I had suffered a brain concussion and a cut over my right eye

I remember waking at midnight, looking up into the eyes of my scared little girl from Reading and then dropping off into blackness again. I awoke in the morning with one of the worst "hangover" effects that I ever hope to have. I could only swallow liquids because I had bitten my tongue so hard that I had left the imprint of my teeth in it.

I was a sad looking apple.

I left the hospital the next day against all judgment and retired to my home for a seven weeks rest in bed. I remember one grand occasion when I had the whole neighborhood talking about me when the ambulance came, and I was carried out on a movable stretcher and taken to the hospital for X-rays. The doctor was still afraid of a fractured pelvic bone and was worried that I would have to be placed in a cast for about six months. However, the X-rays showed nothing was radically wrong, but the doctor was not taking any chances, for just a sliver could be missing, and it would make all the difference in the world.

Once in a while, I helped my mother with her gray hair by getting up and struggling around, but soon I was pronounced okay to go back to school.

I had already missed seven-and-one-half weeks, and I was worried that I would not be allowed to finish. Carrying twenty hours almost proved too much for me, which included one night a week, but I made it and was graduated with my class in April 1943.

After a few more weeks of rest and awaiting my orders for the Navy, I decided to go to work at the Standard Aircraft Company doing the job of shipping clerk and playing softball for them on the side. This lasted all summer, although I was given a scare once in July when the Navy threatened to send me to Ohio Wesleyan in Delaware, Ohio for V-12 training. In other words, I was again starting college.

I notified Chicago about the error and sat back and waited for my new orders. I received them in September and found out that I was being sent to Notre Dame in South Bend for Midshipman training.

My last days at home were spent entirely doing nothing but just being with the folks. Meanwhile, I had also learned that two college mates of mine were both going to Notre Dame, and we made plans to go together.

September 29th finally arrived, and everyone available went down to the railroad station to see us off.

Little did we know what we were getting in for because all we could see ahead of us were four long months of naval training and, beyond that, we didn't give too much thought. We had begun Navy thinking: Get the present job over, and then worry about the next one.

We were excited as kids as we boarded the train that would take us to Chicago and, from there, to South Bend to begin our training. It was the beginning of a long, new, different life. In it, I was to learn many things. One of the most important, I believe, was in the category of self-preservation, of learning to take care of myself. I would also learn the problems and importance of responsibility. I had not, until this time, been introduced to it.

Yes, it all seemed new and exciting, for it was different, so different, that I could not begin to realize where it would lead me in the next four months. I could only guess as to what lay ahead.

Chapter Two

MIDDIE SCHOOL

We arrived in Chicago around seven in the morning on September 30th and had to wait for a train to South Bend, but there were many waiting for the same train so I didn't have too much to worry about. We finally left on the "old rattler," which was to make South Bend very "famous" with the Midshipmen. We arrived in South Bend to be greeted by a host of trucks on which we were loaded, bag and baggage, for the trip to our new home for the next four months.

My first impression of Notre Dame was one of real beauty and still is. The first structure that I remember seeing was the famous Golden Dome of the Administration Building glinting in the autumn sun. Recalling the picture of the campus, it is one of neatness and planning. Looking west from Rockne Memorial, which was at one end and centered, one could see many buildings on either side with a huge lawn separating them.

On the right was, first, the large cafeteria and then two modern V-12 dorms. On the left, forming a square "C" was Lyons Hall, then Morrissey, Howard, and lastly, Badin. On down to the left were some of the classrooms, mostly concerned with science, and, back a ways from the main walk, was Sacred Heart Chapel and the Golden Dome. Farther down toward the stadium, another small quadrangle of buildings were formed, which included the gymnasium, drug store, and post office. Across from these was the huge ordnance hall with all types of guns and cannon mounted inside. Directly to the right of this hall and down about one-fourth of a mile, was the huge Notre Dame stadium. In all, there must have been twenty to twenty-four buildings of all types, but not having much to do with them, I have forgotten their names.

As we arrived, we were lined up in front of Morrissey Hall, and muster was called. As we answered to our name, we were told what hall we belonged in. As I answered, I heard Lyons as the reply.

Lyons Hall contained all of the specialists or trainees for the supply corps. I retired to Lyons and was assigned a room, which I found, after lugging my luggage up three decks, that I was situated on the top floor. My number was one of the big corner rooms, and I found as I entered, that I had three roommates: Paul Sheehan of Boston, Jack Sievl of Bellingham, Washington, and Carl Shannon of Carson City, Nevada. We all found in a hurry that we were good friends.

After noon chow, we went after our uniforms and, being loaded down with them, we were told to go after our books. Somehow the load was carried back to our room and then we received instructions on how to fold our clothes and stow our gear. We then received our schedule for studies, which we found would begin the next day. So, with the thought of bell-bottom trousers and the blue-ringed sailor caps, we went to bed with many thoughts on our mind for the first night.

I shall never forget the four of us in the first morning at reveille. All four of us jumped at the same time to get out of our sacks at the early hour of ten minutes until six. It was dark when we dove into our gym clothes and ran down three decks to be greeted by the early morning fall mist for our exercises. Calisthenics at six in the morning is at first brutal when one is not used to it, but we soon became accustomed to it, and most of us enjoyed it, for it gave us a healthier feeling and better appetite.

After exercises, we went back to our room and began to clean it up and get dressed. First our bunks, then a bit of sweeping, and then we got dressed to go to breakfast. We lined up by sections formed in alphabetical order and marched to the cafeteria with a hup, two, three, four all the way.

After chow in the morning, we roamed back to the hall and collected our books and waited for the bell that would call us to our first class of the day. At the sound, we would again line up beside the building by sections and, at the sound of a bugle, we would all begin to march to the administrative building for classes with a hup, two, three, four.

Usually, four classes were held in the morning, then a break for chow and then the familiar hup, two, three, four would take us to three classes in the afternoon, after which we were usually employed in athletics. Here is a typical day:

First: ORD
Second: SEAMAN
Third: DAM C
Fourth DRILL
Fifth: DRILL
Sixth: STUDY
Seventh: NAV
Eighth: ATH

"ORD" refers to Ordnance, SEAMAN to Seamanship, DAM. C. to Damage Control, NAV to Navigation, and ATH to Athletics. The drills were usually ordnance, seamanship, which included semaphore, blinker and flag hoists, and damage control. Naturally, this schedule contained changes with each day, but it is an example of the week.

Saturdays we had liberty from noon until one o'clock Sunday morning, and we were off Sunday morning at eight until six (I mean 1800 hours) Sunday night. This wasn't much, and as we went out, we certainly learned to enjoy ourselves in a hurried fashion. The four of us were usually together, although Paul neither smoked nor drank, but the other three made up for him. We had some good songfests over beer at the Brandywine Bar next to the LaSalle Hotel. All we did on weekends was drink beer and let off steam. Then back to the grind on Monday.

I had been there but two weeks when I was jolted with the fact that I was being transferred from the "S" group to the "G" classification, which had found themselves entombed in Badin Hall, which the school had condemned six years before. Almost tearfully, I gathered my belongings, for the four of us had learned to get along very well together. I reported to Lt. Callabro, and I made him think he was an Admiral the way I sirred him. I reported to my new room around the corner from the office and found, in comparison to the almost immaculate room in Lyons that I was now in a dirty, small, old looking room. My one roommate was Robert Shattuck from Grand Rapids, Michigan. We became casual friends and remained so throughout the term. But soon I learned that there are many smiles and just as good a man in the "slums" as there are in "riches." Next to us was a Todd Shirley from Enid, Oklahoma, and John Sheehan from Boston. Todd was still fighting the Civil War but found himself entirely surrounded by Yankees.

The new schedule began, and this included a great deal more of Navigation because Supply Officers do not need to know Navigation as well as Deck Officers. This left me always behind in Navigation. But Section 45 was one in which everyone helped everyone else. No better section existed! I soon became its section leader. This was my first "promotion." Next came the Battalion Staff because the job was given to someone with the loudest mou—voice. I was Chief Mustering Petty Officer.

Days passed swiftly, and after the first month, we were no longer regarded as Apprentice Seamen but as Midshipmen. This brought a bigger laundry bill and more contributions to the Red Cross.

In mid-November, my girlfriend from Dayton came up for the weekend, and Bill Roberts, from down at the other end of the unsinkable Badin, was also expecting his girl from Illinois and we planned to make it a foursome. Bill's girl did not make it, but he came along anyway. During the evening at the Oliver Hotel Bar, my girl suddenly stated that Bill needed a date and that she would get one for him. So he agreed. My girl picked out a nice looking young lady from across the room and over she came after some hesitating persuasion. She introduced herself as Peggy, and I didn't catch the last name. But she was very cute. She was from Saint Mary's College across the lake from Notre Dame.

I thought nothing of it at the time and went back to my studies for another week, but the next Saturday, as I was again passing through the Oliver Bar, I encountered the young lady and a friend of mine having a drink together.

I immediately sat down and proceeded to talk for three hours and threatened Peggy that I was going to call her on the following day, which I did. I agreed to meet her in the afternoon, around two, near the highway, where I found her chaperoned. The girl friend soon left, however. We walked through the first snow at Notre Dame to Morrissey Hall to listen to a concert. We didn't say too much, but timidly held hands and watched the skaters on the lake.

I do not believe that all afternoon as we listened to the radio that we said more than ten words, but we just sat and smiled at each other. Some people call it human lightning, others like myself name it love at first sight, but we both felt something happening to each of us. At the end of the program, we walked silently back toward Saint Mary's.

It was the strangest date I ever had. On the way back, we stopped by the cemetery, smiled, and kissed.

We were both lost from that moment on.

[Mary here. I must interrupt because there are some facts, from my mother's side of the story, that my father was unaware of until years later. He has the timing a little off. He certainly had been attracted to Peggy from their first meeting [that was in October] but although he seemed to show up when she was on a date, he never asked her out. Peggy confessed her frustration to her German teacher and confidante, Sister Magdalita – in German. My mother was a German major, an interesting choice during the war, and the only student in her class. During her senior year, the nun and student would simply walk around campus and have normal conversations in German. Sister Magdalita was a good friend of the college's president, Sister Madeleva, who was then a nationally known figure – a noted poet, a spiritual adviser to stars Helen Hayes and Irene Dunne. She also helped scholars fleeing the Nazis to find an academic home as they settled into this country.

Saint Mary's College was also the mother house for the Sisters of the Holy Cross, and they held a Novena to the Blessed Mother every evening at the close of their day. Sister Magdalita mentioned Peggy's wish to Sister Madeleva, who added the petition to the Novena. Sisters always added their own petitions; I don't know how many asked to have a man ask one of the students out. But for about a month, the Sisters prayed that Pat Sheeran would ask Peggy Vlossak out on a date.

It took a few weeks, but there he was, in mid-November, walking up to Saint Mary's formidable LeMans Hall one November Sunday morning. When he asked to see Peggy Vlossak, the nun at the door asked him why, and he said that he'd like to take her to Mass. The result of the Novenas? Or a canny notion on my dad's part that he could get the nuns' approval by taking Peggy to Mass? Whichever was his motive, that didn't work. The nuns were protective; these midshipmen would be here today and gone tomorrow and besides, as Sister of the Door told him, Saint Mary's students had to attend Sunday Mass at Saint Mary's. No exceptions.

Peggy had flown down the four flights (students could not use the elevators during the war) for she and her friends had seen Pat come up the walk. She arrived to find Pat looking a little desperate. And just then, after what seemed to be his last attempt to charm Sister of the Door, Sister Magdalita and Sister Madeleva walked into the hallway. Sister Magdalita took in the scene and went over to the anxious Peggy. "Is he the one?" she whispered, and Peggy nodded. Sister Magdalita nodded to Sister Madeleva, who said, "That's all right, Sister. She can go. I'll be responsible for the consequences."

And that's how they had their first date - Mass in South Bend followed by breakfast, and probably that concert. And, as Dad said, they tried to be together as much as their schedules could allow. And now, back to Dad's story. The next voice you read is Ed's – but you can call him Pat.]

For the remainder of the term, I was floating; my average came down to a 2.95 from 3.15 in one month. Christmas and New Year's arrived finding me spending the holidays at the school. The holidays were preceded by a two-day visit by my mother, who was duly impressed with the routine of the school.

Peg went home for Christmas, and I called her long distance every night, and we wrote an average of three letters a day. She came back early on the 29th of December. I shall never forget that day as long as I live. I called her at the Pfaff home and agreed to meet her at the Grotto in half an hour. I arrived first, waited, and was soon to see a taxi pull up, stop, a young lady emerge, pay her fare, and walk swiftly toward the Grotto. Not seeing me, she swiftly knelt and uttered a prayer with the villain sneaking silently up behind her. She heard, and in a moment, we were together.

After a moment of silence, I led her to the little log chapel, where I made up my mind in a hurry. I asked her to marry me, she consented, and I gave her my college ring, and we held our hearts in our eyes for a few minutes.

Then I saw her to the bus, realizing that I was engaged to this pretty girl, and I had not said more than fifty words to her since I met her. In fact, I couldn't even pronounce her last name. I was baffled but completely happy.

On the evening of New Year's Day, we spent the time together at a friend's home and had a happy time. We were together from then on, even if it could only be but a brief fifteen minutes or less.

January was passing, and I was still in the school, but studies were getting harder and concentration had to be placed on final examinations coming on the 17th and 18th. Those were big days. I remember the last days of marching, studying, and playing on the weekend. The school term was almost over, and to our recollection, it had hardly begun.

Graduation Day, January 20th, at Notre Dame found me in a memory mood about the past four furious months. I had made new friends. I had learned new things. I had fathomed a new life. But most of all, I was taught that no matter who you are, or what you do, the only way to completely satisfy yourself that you have done a good job is to do it yourself. The value paralleling your own work is unlimited. As the day progressed and we were all decked out in our new Ensign blues, we felt very proud that we had survived the now laughed at ordeal. One could see that we were proud as we marched toward the auditorium to be sworn in. We were straighter with more chest expansion. We were happy. We had completed a job which we thought of as well done. I remember the oath, I remember the diploma, and I remember the end. I rushed out of the auditorium throwing my good wishes over my shoulder as I joined Peggy out front to take her home and show her off to the folks.

It was a very self-satisfied officer of the United States Navy and his fiancé who stepped aboard the train that would give them each five days of happiness at home.

Chapter Three

GO WEST, YOUNG MAN

I spent the five days at home displaying my uniforms and my girl. I had already given her the news that my orders read that I was going overseas immediately. I kept it from my mother, but intuition has a way of finding out that something behind the scenes is going on. She knew. From the time that I had been given the news at Notre Dame, I knew that I was getting to be more serious about the war because it was concerning me. Also, I was beginning to think of others more often.

We had fun on my short leave, but Peg went back to school wondering if she would ever see me again. My last day at home was spent with the folks and my sister. I can remember the almost silent ride to the terminal. We were all speaking with our hearts. I was leaving for San Francisco and had to be there by the 31st of January. I shall never forget the goodbyes on that occasion. I still taste the sweet tears of my mother and the tense lips of my sister. My father's handshake did not say goodbye, but it had the feeling that it would welcome me back when all was over. I left leaving my heart all over the place.

Next stop, Chicago and it was my second trip to the big city since the World's Fair of 1933. I found myself with twelve hours to "kill" before the train left for San Francisco. First, I remember, I sent wires home and to Peg to tell them that I had reached this point in one piece. I then proceeded to see three motion pictures and consume five beers at a fashionable hotel bar before I decided that I would wander back to the railroad station, hoping to find some of the fellows there and drown my loneliness. I was completely bewildered when I arrived to find myself with only ten minutes to catch the train. I had forgotten the difference of an hour between train and standard time. Ed Slote dragged me to our car and off we went before I had a chance to attend to anything. The three days on the train were spent in sleeping, eating, and reading, with the exception of the first night, when I serenaded the club car with not only my voice but my imitation of musical instruments. The trip was very pleasant, and we marveled at the beauty of the western lands as we rolled onward.

Finally, after three days, we pulled into Oakland, California and were transferred from the train to the ferry. What a mighty picture: the skyline of San Francisco irregularly breaking the horizon with mammoth buildings and bridges. The bay clogged with ships. The toot-toot of tugging tugs. The rumbling whisper of the machine age in the big city. It was a magnificent sight as we chug-chugged our way over to the San Francisco side of the separating bay. On landing, Ed Slote, Dick Schaub, All Schraff, and I made our way to the Whitcomb Hotel on famous Market Street, where we were to stay for a total of three weeks.

I recall the first trip we made, and that was to the Top of the Mark, the famous bar on top of the Mark Hopkins Hotel overlooking the city. It was quite impressive. Our host was sunny California, and we were out to see the sights. We went sightseeing, dancing, and barring. We visited the Junior Officer's Club and found some nice girls and made our contact with the city in that manner. We saw the campus of the University of California at Berkeley and took three sorority girls to the Claremont Hotel overlooking the bay and the Golden Gate Bridge. On one weekend, we rented a car to show off at Stamford University at Palo Alto but found that we had the smallest car in the place. After a brief sojourn in the cadaver plant (Al found a medical student), we visited a den bar on the outskirts with three of the college belles. We only rode cable cars in 'Frisco once. We went to shows with the J.O.C. girls and had so much fun that the three of us had to get an advance in pay to take care of our jesting. Once I felt very proud of myself and that happened when I sent a dozen roses to Peg on Valentine's Day. She was slaving back at dear old Saint Mary's. I began missing her more and more and liking it.

We reported in at the Federal Building every other day to find out any developments. Finally, the day arrived when we were notified that we would soon leave the continental limits of the good old U.S.A. We telephoned home, and by our voices, they knew that it would be quite some time before they would hear from us again. We assembled our gear, and on February 23, 1944, we reported aboard ship, the U.S.S. President Polk, for transportation westward to find the Commander of the Third Fleet. We spent our last night ashore getting a haircut and going to bed in the Whitcomb for the last time. Dawn found us hunting a cab to take us to our ship for the beginning of the big adventure that lay ahead of us.

It was a sad group that raised their heads to watch the Golden Gate Bridge directly over us, behind us, and finally disappearing in the dismal fog. We were on our way.

Chapter Four

PACIFIC SAILING

Sailing from San Francisco began in the late afternoon of February 24, 1944. The lights of the city became very fascinating as they twinkled and sputtered and finally disappeared with the historical Golden Gate Bridge in the dusk and fog. We had an overnight trip to San Diego to take on some very important cargo: five thousand Marines. We enjoyed liberty in San Diego for a day, although some gal almost had me thrown out for using the word "queer" in our conversation. I was glad to return to the ship for the night's sleep in preparation for the long journey ahead of us. The three of us were up at the crack of reveille to breakfast and watch the ship unmoor. We went down to the dock to feel U.S.A. soil for the last time, and I happened to run into Jim Arata of Xavier football fame, now a Marine Second Lieutenant, and we jabbed the gab until it was time for the ship to get underway.

It was a very conflicting and struggling feeling that I combated as the ship pulled away, and we were off for sure now. Even then, we were beginning to pray for some miracle to end the war. One to two days out from the California coast find the water a bit rough. We began to experience our first "sea legs" as we rolled from side to side walking down passageways. Dinner the first evening was spent sliding from table to table. No one became sick. We were having too much fun to think about it. The voyage finally settled down to a little short of monotonous as claustrophobia began to set in. We played cards and read once in a while and sometimes battered the piano into worse condition than it was, but finally, the restlessness was noted by the Captain, and he put us on security watch. That meant that we took care of the Marines. We had one submarine scare that proved to be a splendid laxative for all who needed one, but it was a false alarm.

We passed one ship, which amazed me, for I thought that we were on the slowest in the Navy. We passed over the equator, but we were not duly initiated as were other unfortunates on other ships.

Finally, on the seventeenth day, we sighted land. Behold: New Caledonia. We were pulling into the capital city, which was Noumea. What a disappointing sight. New Caledonia, by the way, is just east of Australia and was untouched by war, although air raid precautions had been taken. We disembarked and were driven to the interior of the island to a receiving station, where we were given a bunk in one of the many Quonset huts. The station had an excellent mess and during the evening meal, we were entertained by a Negro trio.

Al Schraff, Dick Schaub, and I stayed in Noumea awaiting transportation for sixteen days and had ourselves a good time. The Pacifique Club and the Ansa Vata Beach Club, where we spent most of our time, were somewhat different than we were used to, but we learned soon enough that we had to do a lot more than be without a few beers once in a while. We played football on the beach, swam in the ocean, and went to a few dances as "stragglers." The city was somewhat picturesque in that the downtown section was mostly downtrodden shacks with a fairly nice small wooden building that operated as a City Hall. Every day, the three of us thumbed a ride to the Post Office downtown to receive our mail, and we did get quite a bit, which proved to be a very great surprise for the three of us. Once, poor Al didn't get a letter from his best girl for four days, and he was worried sick. But all was well, finally.

The sea in this part of the world was one of the calmest and smoothest I had ever seen. The sun shone through the day, even when the one-minute showers appeared. It was a quiet "I'll do it tomorrow" town. Most of the inhabitants were French with a bunch of Blacks thrown in.

We usually stayed on the base in the afternoon and early evening, eating chow and sometimes seeing a movie on the hill overlooking the camp. One day, a Sunday, I was in heaven for I saw a baseball game in which Bob Feller was supposed to have pitched. The caliber of the rest of the players was excellent, but I was disappointed that Feller did not show up, due to hospitalization for a minor injury. The game was the "World Series" between the Army and the Navy in this theatre. I enjoyed the whole game, which ended in a victory for the Army.

Finally, we were advised that our sailing date was soon to become reality. We had enjoyed our first island visit. What proved to be our last day in town was spent in gathering souvenirs to send home. That evening, we went out to dinner, and I was informed at the table that I had missed the first ship out that afternoon. On returning to the base, I checked at the office and found out that they could not locate me, and it was a short notice, but that I was to sail the next day for Guadalcanal, the place I had read so much about in the newspapers but never thought I would see. I retired to my quarters to begin packing. In the meantime, Dick had been sent to the hospital for a back ailment, spending five months on the island, while Al was due to sail with me, although he was assigned to another ship.

The following morning found us down at the dock with, of course, nothing being done about it. After a few small delays in the rain, we were loaded aboard a small boat and sent out into the bay. We reported aboard the U.S.S. Elmore for our transportation. It was an APA (attack ship). It was smaller than the Polk, but we didn't have the great number of passengers that we had on the Polk. Smith and Steddom, Midshipman friends, who had recently arrived in Noumea, were also assigned to the Elmore. Our quarters were two feet above the keel next to the engine room, so we thought. It was too hot for comfort. Out came cots that we had procured in San Francisco and dragged all over the Pacific, and we went to sleep topside on deck. It was delightful. The chow aboard was not as good as the Polk's mess, and we were restricted from the wardroom except for Mess Call, but we didn't mind for the trip was to take but five days. We were the second ship in a convoy of five, the biggest I had seen.

We were headed for the equator and Guadalcanal. We were headed for war.

Chapter Five

SHIP HUNTING

The sun was shining brightly, as it had a habit of doing in this section, as we pulled into a small bay surrounded by a group of islands. The famous Guadalcanal was on our port side (I was beginning to get "salty" at last) and what a disappointment it was. Naturally, being fresh out of the States, I had expected something of better hospitality. New Caledonia had been a disappointment but, compared to Guadalcanal, it was a paradise. Guadalcanal was either all mud or dust.

We were unloaded into an LCVP (a shoe box with a motor) and taken to the beach to be followed by our gear in another boat. Loaded on trucks, we were taken to the Officer's section of the island. Another bunk in another Quonset hut. However, the stay here proved to be rather short. We began to notice how existence on an island survived from all that was not "USA caliber." Coconut palms dotted the island as far as the eye could see, but inland, the island was blessed with a larger and finer tree, somewhat on the order of a spreading elm. Mud was everywhere. Showers were taken in public, and latrine use was semi-public, pointing out the fact that few females were present. Dirt roads led everywhere and nowhere. On one short trip, we found a large landing strip that had gained some fame as Henderson Field. But the existence was monotonous, and we found that most of the men stationed here were trying to do their best to fight it by doing new things and redoing the old. Movies were the only recreation, with the exception of slapping determined mosquitoes. We were stationed in Hut #7 with two Catholic priests who kept our morale up with hilarious stories. We walked three miles a day for chow.

Each day, we checked at the sailing office if we were the next to leave for points unknown. On the third day, we found out that we were to be sent farther, fifty miles exactly, to a spot on the map known as the Russell Islands. We were to be transported by an APC, which were used in these parts as mail boats. At the moment, we did not know what these "ships" were like, so expressed no opinion on the mode of transportation, but the next morning, after packing, we went down to the dock to see our "ship" roll in. Approximately eighty feet in length with a fifteen foot beam, it was like a small yacht with a superstructure. There were only seven of us reporting aboard for the jaunt to the Russells, but we enjoyed it immensely. It was a compact "big" ship. We really enjoyed this cruise and would have been glad to get it as duty.

We landed at the Russells after a five-hour trip with no one, not even a welcoming committee, to greet us. We soon procured a truck to take us to our newly assigned quarters at the top of a hill. We arrived in time to witness a USO show that tickled our funny bones for there were a couple of gals in it that were really taking a beating, not only from the actors, but the audience as well. After the show was over, we reported to the Commanding Officer present as the Commanding Officer absent was dancing with one of the nurses stationed at the hospital. It was late. We had a big chow while talking with the officer who gave us our choice of LCIs (landing craft infantry) or LSTs (landing ship, tank or tank landing ship) at this meeting. I was the only one to choose an LCI, which I naturally received, although I wasn't sure what the devil they were. Two of the seven received LSTs, and the rest were content with the second choice. We were given quarters wherever they could be found for that night, and Al and I ended up in the dispensary on the softest beds I have ever slept on in the Navy. We were equipped with the latest funnies (six weeks previous) and finally settled down to a good night's sleep.

In the morning, we were again loaded on the APC and taken to our final destinations: the Florida Islands. We arrived on the 12th of April, late in the afternoon and, not finding anyone to report our presence, attended the movie up the road. After the show, we were guided with scorn (for not mustering in) to the Commanding Officer, Commander Smith, whom I did not recognize as a Commander, not hearing his rank stated and proceeded to stand with the greatest of ease throughout his welcome, while the other six stood at something close to attention. I was afraid that I had offended him with my easy manner, but nothing was said, and relieved, I left to take my orders to the clerk's office. Lt. Loban endorsed my orders and assigned me to the U.S.S. LCI (L) 331 for duty. It was too late to report aboard that night, so the seven of us slept ashore in a Quonset hut equipped with a party that kept me from getting any sleep.

[Note: LCI stands for Landing Craft Infantry, commonly called "Elsies." They were developed especially for WW2 and used to land large numbers of infantry directly onto the beaches. Some 923 were built for both Pacific and European theaters.]

The next morning found us looking for a small boat to take us to our respectively assigned ships. Having procured one after a two-hour search, we made the rounds of the bay, which gave me my first good look at an LCI. To me, they looked good. All the other fellows found their ships, but I could not locate the 331, so back to the base I went to discover that it was on an operation at an island called Emirau and would not return for a couple of weeks. I was reassigned to LCI 357 and again made my way back to Hutchinson Creek, where there were about thirty LCIs lined up on the beach. Spotting the 357, I made my way aboard with my gear and proceeded to find someone who could set me right. I knocked on the Exec's cabin to find that both the Executive and Engineering Officers were in the familiar spot that I was soon to learn to enjoy and that was the good old sack. Lt (jg) Simmons and Ensign Czygledi greeted me with open arms and informed me that the Skipper would be back in a short time. Upon his return, I was introduced to Lt (jg) Evers, who was a tall, humorous fellow. He assigned me to the troop officer's quarters, which were spacious and comfortable and then proceeded in the next two weeks to indoctrinate me to LCI life. I was made the Chief Censor and Watch Stander (while in port) aboard.

The two weeks aboard the 357 were spent in eating good chow, seeing movies, playing ball, and for one three-day stretch went out on maneuvers with ten other ships. This really excited me for it was the first time that I was on a "steaming" LCI. I handled the ship for a brief period of five minutes and received quite a thrill out of it. I backed full, went ahead standard, rotated quads, and had a good time for myself.

The first night on maneuvers was spent in anchoring near a small island by the name of Malaita, where I had my first opportunity to barter with the natives. What a ribbing I received when I gave two packs of cigarettes for a small necklace (made in New Zealand). My face was red at the mention of the word "necklace" for the remainder of the trip. After Corpens, Formations, Turns, and everything else in shipboard seamanship, we made our way to the home base and pulled into the now familiar Hutchinson Creek to find the good old 331 had arrived and was now in dry dock.

I waited aboard the 357 until the 331 came out of dry dock and then met the Captain, Lt (jg) Van Vleck, who told me to report aboard as soon as possible. The same night, I packed, and after a few timid adios, made my way down the shore to the 331. What a difference in ships! The 357 was the newer type, while the 331 was the older type and had been in service much longer. I made my way up the landing ramp at ten that night and was escorted into the wardroom of the ship I was destined to stay aboard for the rest of my overseas service. I made my way into the wardroom to meet my new shipmates.

I had reported aboard my ship, two months to the day after I had left the States.

Chapter Six

LCI LIFE

I entered the wardroom occupied by three officers. One light was burning. It was a small room filled with tobacco smoke. In the dim light, I recognized the Skipper, whom I had met earlier in the day. He welcomed me aboard and introduced me to the other two, who proved to be Ensigns Jim Hofmann of Cleveland, Ohio and Don Heltzel of Warren, Ohio. Jim was the Exec and Don was Engineering Officer. After a few moments of kicking the breeze, I was given a reporting aboard present. Twenty letters from home. What a thrill. It had been quite some time since I had heard from home, and I was really missing it. The Skipper, Van, had taken over the ship the same day I had come aboard, and he went about his business while I read the good word from home and Peg. Soon equipped with an old Navy standby, a cup of coffee, I finished reading and settled back for a few minutes talking with the rest of the fellows. I soon admitted that I was a bit on the weary side and wished to sack in. I was led by the Stewart's Mate to #2 hold for the night until better accommodations could be made. I spent a lonely night attempting to register an accounting of what lay ahead, but I soon dropped off to a very welcome sleep.

Early the next morning, I was awakened for breakfast by the Stewart's Mate and made my way to the wardroom for my early morning wash. I found that the occupants of the wardroom were still enjoying their happy slumber, so I went ahead and ordered my hot cakes (which soon became a ritual) and settled down for my first breakfast.

When the ship "turned to," we prepared to get underway to take on water. We proceeded to Tulagi Island and beached. The hoses went over the bow while the ramps were lowered for the new Supply and Commissary Officer to go ashore and draw provisions. The cook and

I, along with a small working party, soon brought back a tremendous amount of stores and supplies. It was a trip in the mud for just a short distance until we came upon the warehouse stored ceiling high with cases of food. After making out the available list that we wished to draw for that day, we waited for a truck to come along and then proceeded to pile the cases on and returned to the ship where the ship's crew made a long passing chain to get the supplies aboard. After they were stored in #4 hold and the hoses were secured after taking on ten thousand gallons of fresh water, we pulled off the beach, or in Navy lingo, retracted, and meandered through the submarine nets back to Hutchinson Creek. The submarine nets enclosed Tulagi from the outer bay.

After beaching, I began my duties by supervising the galley. It was very small, and the cramped quarters did not give the cook much room to move around in. He had a sink, coffee urn, and working table on one side, and the small diesel oil stove on the other. The dishes and trays were stored in a small wooden cabinet next to the stove. We also rigged up a Mess table on the outside for working purposes. We had, at the time, a seaman cook for our regular cook was being transferred to the good old USA, and we were trying to get another for duty. My other duties at the moment concerned equipping the ship so that everyone would feel at home, at least, so it seemed according to the various and many items that I was supposed to invent from cloud pulling.

Meanwhile, I became acquainted with some of the crew members, and they began to show me the rounds of the ship. The men took a liking to me and I to them. They began to show me the various routines and the manner of operating aboard an LCI. At the time, there was a complement of four officers and thirty enlisted men aboard.

I found that the ship was, approximately, one hundred and fifty seven feet long and had a 23-foot beam. The forecastle (pronounced folk-sill) to the bow of the ship was above the main deck by three feet. The #1 gun, a 20mm, was housed here. Bulwarks along the main deck divided the main deck from the passageways leading up from the ramps, one on each side of the ship. The passageways extended aft to #3 and #4 gun tubs. The bulwarks, or short walls, led back to within five feet of the superstructure. The superstructure, or deck house, held the Captain's quarters at main deck level. Directly above was the pilot house from where the ship was steered. Above the pilot house was the bridge or conning tower where the Officer of the Day (OOD) stood his underway watch. The whole section rose up to a height of nearly eighteen feet. Directly behind the pilot house was the weather deck, which was used for lounging, but also contained the #2 gun, which was a 20mm automatic machine gun. Canvas covered this deck from the elements. Inside the deck house, from the Captain's quarters, one walked back toward the stern of the ship finding first, the radio room on the immediate left; back through a small passageway passing the ladder going up to the deck above and continuing back about fifteen feet to the wardroom on the left, which also held the Officer's Head or washroom. On turning to the left to enter the wardroom, another ladder was passed that led down to the deck below that housed most of the crew members. It was a small compartment. Continuing back toward the stern of the ship was the galley and then the crew's head and shower room. That comprised the interior of the ship. Outside on deck, aft, were the #3 and #4 gun tubs, also 20MMs, and the stern anchor winch, which was a small gasoline engine that was used to haul in the 750-pound anchor. Returning into the deck house by the crew's head was another ladder leading down into the bowels of the ship that found at the bottom, the power or engine room. There were eight 6-71 Diesel engines in two quads of four each that enabled the ship to attain a speed of fifteen knots at flank speed. This speed was very seldom, if ever, used. There were four holds plus the crew's quarters in the ship. #1 hold was forward near the bow and just aft of the boatswain's locker, which was located in the bow of the ship and contained all of the deck gear that could be stowed there. #2 hold was just forward of the conning tower, and #3 hold was below the Captain's quarters extending aft. This hold was also used for a crew's quarters. #4 hold was behind the deck house, and the ladder leading down to the hold was beside #3 and #4 guns. This hold was the storeroom for commissary and supply stores and also held the small ammunition magazine and emergency steering room. This, with of course, many added accessories, which will be mentioned later, outlined the ship. The ship was used for a small troop transport and could house two hundred Army soldiers.

The ship made up a baseball team, and we had weekly games on the beach. Almost all the men who could go would attend the movies every night on the beach near the base offices, which was around the island in the rear of the housing creek. There was an Officer's Club, which I never saw the inside of, across the bay from the base and had the ironic name of the Iron Bottom Bay Club. It overlooked the bay where a number of our large fighting ships were nestled in the shadows of the hills. The weather in this part of the world was delightful. Showers were few and not too heavy. It was lazy summer all year.

I didn't handle the ship much, just once, and that scared everyone but me. I knew I didn't know what I was doing. But I brought the ship up the beach, turned her into shore, and beached her, which also called for the letting go of the stern anchor. It wasn't a bad job, but I couldn't find anyone to agree with me.

Most of the days for the next month were spent in learning the operation of the ship, my various duties, and becoming acquainted with the rest of the Officers on the other ships. Al Schraff was aboard the 336. Slote was aboard the 66, which was a gunboat that was equipped with a three-inch gun on the main deck. Some of my lesser acquaintances were spread around the flotilla, which operated under the Third Fleet and was tabbed Flotilla Five. It was under the leadership of Commander Smith.

Early in May, we began to hear rumors that the whole flotilla was to be transferred to another theatre of operations, and we finally heard that this was true. We were destined to sail for New Guinea in the middle of May. All of the supplies, stores, water, and fuel were taken on for the expected trip, which would lead us from the quiet solitude of a rear base into the thick of the fighting that I had almost forgotten.

Some of the crew members that I had grown to know quite well included two good signalmen, Craver and Devore; the college quartermaster, Holcomb; Theetge of Cincinnati along with Ely and Stidham of the "black gang;" Hillman, the prejudiced Mississippian; Stec and Orlando, boatswain's mates; Toms, the "cook;" and little Robert Lee Nunley, the happy-go-lucky Stewart's Mate.

Most of the men, like myself, were soon to learn the knack of ducking at the right time. Little did we know that our ship was to be part of the coming rage against the Japs in the new offensive that the higher-ups had thought up for us to take part in.

The war was getting closer.

Chapter Seven

NEW JUNGLES

I was given a nervous stomach condition a few days before sailing to our new base. The Skipper informed me that I was to stand watch with the rest of the officers. Now, I had never kept a ship in column, and I was somewhat tense and a bit scared that I would do something wrong. I had handled the ship rarely up to now.

The day arrived when the entire flotilla was broken up, and we made preparations to get underway and form up in columns as previously planned by the Commander and the Captains at their meetings. I recall the day as calm and delightful for a cruise. The trip was to last three-and one-half days.

My first watch was the 1600-2000 watch, which we dogged. In other words, two officers stood this watch, one from four to six and the other from six to eight at night. This eliminated the possibility of always getting the same watch.

I relieved the Skipper at a quarter to four, but since the columns were still forming, he stayed up to help me in my obvious dilemma. My first watch didn't last long because we had chow at 1630, and I was relieved at a quarter of five to eat mine. But my next watch came about at midnight until four in the morning. My first watch, and it happened to be the midwatch. It was a "honey."

First of all, I must explain that ships were sure to gain or lose a bit of distance because of the variations at different speeds of the ship's engines. On the conn, we had a small buzzer that enabled us to signal the engine room. One buzz meant an increase of ten RPMs (Revolutions per Minute) and two buzzes decreased the speed by Ten RPMs. This was necessary because when ships were in column, speed increases or decreases could not be as much as 50 or 100 RPMs. This would cause too much confusion in the column. It was fairly easy to stay in column because we had good helmsmen.

This particular night was very dark with but a few stars and no moon whatsoever. I remember relieving at a quarter to midnight, awakened from a deep sleep a half an hour earlier. A quick cup of coffee, and I was up the ladder to the conn. My ship's speed and heading were given me on reporting. Then the other officer retired below, and I was on my own. Devore was on watch with me as signalman, and Polcomb was in the pilot house, so I had no worries about the ship being handled the way it should be. On the open-air conning tower were three voice tubes that led down into the pilot house, forming one tube. Its outlet was right beside the helmsman's ear. He was perched on a stool and controlled the helm, which looked like a streetcar motorman's handle control. In column, the helmsman merely had to keep the bow of our ship on the stern of the ship ahead. This wasn't too hard if the water was calm and on this trip, it happened to be.

Around one-thirty, as the watch began to get a bit relaxed, a quick signal, and all of a sudden, before I could notify the Skipper, we were making a sharp right turn (Corpen), which is done by following the "wake" of the ship ahead around a ninety-degree turn to starboard and still staying in column. I tried to bring the ship around, but I overshot my mark a bit and, looking back, I saw that the ship behind me had crept up quite a distance on me. I added a few quick single buzzes, grabbed a flashlight, and began signaling my speed to the ship behind. In the meantime, I tried to get the ship back in column as quickly as I could. The Skipper must have heard or felt my predicament for he came up on the conn and asked me if I was having any trouble. I assured him that this had happened so suddenly that I was not able to send for him and that I had overshot the turn. He smiled and silently left the conn with a calming word to relax and, if I came too close to the ship ahead, to merely pull a bit out of column and then ease back in.

I felt a bit silly now, but at the time it seemed that the ship was in peril. Sheepishly, I went back to watching the movements of the ship ahead. The night slowly passed, and I was finally relieved without any more trouble. Happily, I went below and sat down and mentally surveyed the night. I drank a cup of coffee which somewhat relaxed me, and I felt better. At last, I crawled into my sack over the wardroom table and was asleep in no time.

The rest of the trip was spent in enjoying the scenery for nothing else of importance happened to me on the following watches. I remember the day when we pulled into New Guinea. It was a small and narrow inlet that we had to meander through to come into the real base. The river was very deep and larger ships had no difficulty in coming into the bay, although the largest ships entered from the other side. We formed a single column and wound our way through the pass and came out into a huge body of water that I learned was Milne Bay. We made our way to Stringer Bay, a small amphibious base inside Milne Bay and anchored out from the beach. Immediately, I went ashore with a working party and drew supplies that we were glad to get before the other ships sent in their order. However, the base Supply Officer became rather irritated when I came back again with a new order and asked me to leave. All I did was try and get more strawberries! So sadly, I returned to the ship with my working party to find that we were going to beach. At sundown, all of the ships beached side by side, and the trip was officially ended.

Milne Bay was a base composed of three individual bays as far as we were concerned. Stringer Bay was our headquarters; Ladava, three miles around the bay was where we drew our foodstuffs; Gamadota, where GSK supplies were drawn. GSK signified anything from nails to linoleum. I soon came to hate the long water trip to the mud of Gamadota. It was never dry.

But first, we decided to get acquainted with our part of the base. Movies here were also the main method of entertainment, although, here they were held inside because it rained so much. The beach was rather sandy and led to some jungle growth, but most of it had been cut away. A small brook to our left went through the center of town. A ball diamond was discovered beside the stream, which was used to a great extent when we found a ball and bat. The buildings were all Quonset types, big and small. A beach master ruled the shore and arranged transportation for all working parties. Jeeps were available to officers, but the privilege was abused and soon withdrawn. Although coconut trees predominated, there were other small varieties resembling green redwoods. But it was muddy.

By this time, Don Heltzel and I had become good friends and went everywhere together and were known as "Mutt and Jeff" because of my 6 foot 2 inches against his 5 foot 7 inches. We went to shows at night and explored the island by day. Most of it was the same as the Solomons. Where there were no buildings, there was dense growth and jungle, although there was little danger from wild animals.

At the end of each day, Don and I usually went to a show, while Van met an Army friend and Jim usually stayed aboard. On Sundays, there would be a rush for the ball diamond and a game with some other ship. We fared pretty well in this league as it happened to turn into later. Some Sundays, we celebrated by having dinner with a very fair guest for the day. Van and his Army friend would bring one of the base nurses to dinner and then take her to a show. She seemed like a princess. It was hard to believe that I had been overseas for three months.

The whole flotilla was again broken up when we found out that we were to be transferred to Flotilla Seven. Other ships in Flotilla Five were scattered here and there by twos and threes. Buna, Gona, Alexishafen, and Finschhafen, New Guinea claimed most of them. But we were not in a new flotilla, which was now forming in Milne Bay.

In June, we were still "unattached" and were put on temporary duty of hauling passengers up the line. Our first trip was to take ten Officers and a few enlisted men to Wakde. This proved to be the longest unescorted LCI trip yet taken in the Southwest Pacific, covering five hundred miles. We journeyed up to Cape Cretin, staying close to the shore and hitting its harbor right on the "nose.," After stopping there for a few hours, we cruised farther up the coast through some narrow channels, passing ships in the dead of night. Up to now, we had been darkened at night for all voyages, but here, we had to have running lights because of the narrow passages. Slowly inching our way up the coast of New Guinea proved to be quite a trip for all of the passengers aboard. Most of them lost a bit, however, when Bob, the Stewart's Mate, oiled up his "galloping dominoes" and proceeded to win a few hundred dollars and three good watches. And he kept the officer passengers in stitches with his unconscious humor. He certainly had quite a time for there were fifteen officers in all, and he could only serve five at a time. So he made nine trips a day, usually to the weather deck, where we ate and basked in the sunlight.

During the day, the trip was very enjoyable, due to the warm weather cooled by an excellent sea breeze. We continued on up the New Guinea coast, passing Hollandia, finally arriving at Wakde at 1900 hours. The trip had taken three days. To our dismay, there was no signal tower, and we were not allowed into the bay after sunset. This was a security measure. So we had to circle around and backtrack for five hours, turn and come back. When dawn broke on the following morning, I was on watch and through the haze and disappearing darkness, I saw land dead ahead. It was an island. We turned to port toward Wakde, and the Skipper took over. Upon arriving, the passengers stayed aboard for the day and night during which we heard a broadcast over the radio that New Guinea was now clear of Japanese air raids, only to have an enemy plane come over later in the night and bomb the gasoline dump with two direct hits near the air strip.

The next morning found the passengers disembarking, and we sat around for four days before getting underway to return to Hollandia. We made that port the following day and pulled in to find my old ship, the 357, anchored near a cove. So we proceeded in that direction, and Van let me take her alongside. The 357 had a movie projector aboard, and every night, we had movies and sang songs for the next two weeks. The only time we left their side was to go across the bay to draw water, and then we returned to the 357.

At the end of two weeks, we received orders to return to Milne Bay with more passengers, this time, they were hospital cases. The 338 was also in the bay and destined for Milne, so were also included in the new duty. We loaded up from an LST Hospital Ship and also received some supplies from her after quite an argument. On the afternoon of June 23rd, we sailed from Hollandia. I'll never forget the doctor who reported aboard to take care of the patients on our ship. He took one look at me and said, "Are you one of the patients?" And he meant it.

We hit some fairly rough water on the way down and made an "emergency" landing at Alexishafen to give the patients a rest. One of them was near death from burns received, due to his own misconduct. He had picked up an ignited hand grenade and it went off. It was filled with phosphorous. He received blood transfusions on the ship and beach.

Alexishafen was filled with LCIs from our old flotilla. We had quite a welcome. It was short, however, for we left the same afternoon for Cape Cretin. We arrived there the next morning, and the doctor advised going any further as some of the patients were not doing well at all. We agreed and sympathized with the poor casualties for it had been a rough ride. We disembarked our patients at Cape Cretin on the beach in Langmak Bay where there were some ambulances waiting to take them to the hospital. We stayed here for two days, and I took advantage of the situation and took some of the men to get some chow. We brought back a truckload including fifty strawberry sundaes. We really piled on the fresh and dry provisions here. The next day, we got underway for Milne Bay. This time, we were without passengers. We were on our way to Milne Bay to receive one of the biggest shocks to date, and it meant that we were now to be a ship of action and not one for "pleasure" cruising. We steamed into Milne Bay in July to find that almost all of the ships of our flotilla were already there or, as we later learned, were on their way to be converted for the same type duty.

Commander Day came aboard as we beached and greeted us. He came to the wardroom with us to relax and give us the lowdown on our new duty. Commenting on Commander Day, I can say that I have never met a more nervous man in my life. He was absolutely shaking and chain-smoked. And he loved to look at magazines.

While looking at some of our old *Time* editions, he unraveled the story that, at the time, truly amazed us, and we felt as if we were doomed indeed.

Chapter Eight

CONVERSION

We were destined to become a rocket ship in a short time. I shuddered at the thought because I had already been on a trial run when the flotilla was still at Hutchinson Creek on one of those new-fangled rocket ships. LCI 70 had been loaded down with some of the launchers for experiments at that time and I decided to go along to see what they were. They scared the very devil out of me. And here, not three months later, we were being assigned to the same duty. All of Flotilla Seven in groups 19, 20, and 21 were to be converted at Milne Bay. We, more or less, scoffed at our new assignment because of the novelty of it. Commander Day explained that the ships would be converted at the Destroyer Base near Ladava. Two ships could be worked on at a time and perhaps more. This was to be determined by the time it took the first couple of ships. We were to be the sixth ship worked on.

Meanwhile, we were based at Stringer Bay and with the new ships coming in, we went around and got acquainted with the officers on the other ships. The 338 became our buddies in Goodman, Cantrelle, and Lewis. We went to movies together and had a few beer sessions aboard each other's ship before conversion commenced. I had my duties down fairly well by this time for they usually followed an Order of the Day. The following schedule changed, naturally, with the requirements of the day involved. But it is an example that the leading Petty Officers used as a guide.

ORDER OF THE DAY
1 August, 1944
0630 – Reveille
0700--Breakfast
0730—Sweep down fore and aft
0800—Turn To:
    Deck Force----Wire brush and paint weather deck
    Gunner's Mates-Clean #3 and #4 guns
    Motor Machs----Work on starboard inboard forward engine
    Signalmen-----Fix Signal light. Wire brush ladder
    Radioman------Type up Monthly Reports
1115—Knock off. Sweep down
1130—Noon chow
1300—Turn to as before
1600—Knock off. Sleep down
1800--#1 Liberty party prepared to go ashore
2100—All hands aboard
2200—Taps
        J.H. Hofmann, Ens.
        Executive Officer

After a few more ball games, movies, and working parties that took me endlessly to Gamadota mud for supplies and other necessities, we were notified in the first week of August to stand by to go to the destroyer base for conversion. The work crews at the base found that it was simpler to work on as many ships as possible at a time and any improvisions could be foreseen and corrected for the benefit of the entire flotilla. We got underway the first Sunday in August for the conversion. The job would take approximately five weeks. We made our way to Ladava, a distance of about two miles and tied up at the port side of the dock, in front of a group of three ships, which required excellent ship handling. Our Skipper was quite capable. No one was worried when he had the bridge. We (the four officers) then made out a group of work chits for our respective departments that we thought as urgent and after landing, turned them over to the shore base workshops. These chits were made in duplicate and, when the job was completed, the copy would be returned to us with the word "Completed" stamped on it. However, the job had to have the approval of the Captain before it could be classified as finished.

The second day, I had my first look at our new launchers. There were three types altogether, and we were to get the newest of the three. It was the Mark Eight. Each launcher resembled a metal orange crate with twelve individual racks, three in a row and consisting of four rows. We received a total of 44 launchers. This meant that we could fire a total of 528 rockets in a single loading. Each rocket had the firepower of a five-inch shell. Our new job became clearer day by day. We were to *precede* the first wave of troops into the beach, firing our rockets at timed intervals as we proceeded until all of our rockets were fired. Then, our automatic weapons were turned on the beach. The description of going in before the first wave certainly gave us an air of importance, now that we were a *fighting ship*.

We began to like it here, for staying in one place for a definite period of time, brought our old mail up to date and the new mail became a daily flow. Each day, our crew assembled the launchers and passed them on to the shore base gang to weld on the decks. They were welded, with some clearance from the edge of the ship, to enable another ship to come alongside without damaging them and aligned as to the angle needed for the separate launcher. The first four launchers were aimed dead ahead. The next four at an angle of one-half of a degree outboard. The next group was placed with a bit larger angle outboard and so on until the side of 22 had been welded. Then, work commenced on the other side. The various angles were designed to give the launchers breadth as well as depth on any target. We learned that we could cover about 350 yards of beach. Depth to the target was reached by the forward motion of the ship. In other words, with the ship proceeding at six knots toward the beach, rockets were fired either 22 or 44 at a time. After the first round was fired, there would be a pause of a designated number of seconds before the next round was discharged, enabling the ship to get that much closer to the target and automatically giving the rockets greater depth, although their range was a maximum of twelve hundred yards. The rockets were fired electrically from the conn. The charge was from two batteries in the pilot house.

The day they put the firing switch in intrigued me, and I watched the entire proceedings. On one board, there were two switches, one controlling the port side of the launchers and one the starboard. The switches rotated in a circle, clockwise, on which were numbers from one through twelve. Two safety plugs had to be inserted to enable electrical contact to travel from the batteries to the launchers. The launchers, as stated before, contained twelve trays each. All forty-four launchers had a #1 tray, a #2 tray, and so on through twelve. When the safety plugs had been inserted and firing was ready to begin, the Exec pushed the switches around to one. Contact was made with the #1 tray in each of the forty-four launchers and the rockets in those trays were fired. Then the #2 tray and so on in regular order. No less than twenty-two rockets or more than forty-four could be fired at one time. However, above the switches were four buttons. These buttons controlled our range rockets, four in number. These four rockets were in the #1 launcher on the port and starboard sides. They were placed all loaded up and the crew was at their new battle stations and all was ready. Inter-communications with all guns from the conn were maintained by small earphones and mouthpieces. We were instructed that all was ready, and we neared our objective. Rockets were fired only one or two at a time, for the launchers were not completely filled on our trial run. But I shall never forget those first repercussions. They were earsplitting. After the rockets were fired, the #1 gun and two twin 50's, which had been placed on the bulwark on the main deck, opened up and strafed the beach. We knocked down the sign which was the guide to shoot at, that Commander Day definitely didn't want us to destroy. Nevertheless, he liked the shooting and said nothing. We streamed back for Stringer Bay, which already held five new LCI(R)s. It was here that we received the news that we were not only to be rocket ships but, in addition, to be assigned the task of fire-fighting. Five hundred gallon Chrysler pumps, hoses, nozzles, and other fire-fighting was brought aboard, and a part of the crew was assigned as fire fighters.

At last, in mid-September, when all ships were completed, we got underway and sailed for Normanby Island, about fifty miles distant. We were not to try our rockets, for there were many natives on that island, but we did test our fire-fighting gear. The natives must have thought it a weird sight, indeed, to see a number of small ships steam into the bay, pull up to the beach, and watch about ten men from each

My Log

ship go down a Jacob's ladder over the bow, pulling a long white hose and squirting a couple of trees with water. But we were beginning to get the hang of our new responsibilities. Our stay at Normanby Island lasted three days. I was the one who did not enjoy it. I became ill with a 103 degree fever caused by seven large boils on the small of my back. The pharmacist Mate lanced them, and they soon cleared up, and I was able to resume my duties.

From Normanby, we sailed back to Stringer Bay to await further orders that we knew were soon forthcoming. The last days at Milne Bay were spent in readiness for the coming trip, and we had more recreation, for we did not know when we would get more. When all of the ships were ready and waiting, orders were received to get underway for Hollandia, New Guinea.

We sailed from Milne Bay on September 20, 1944, one month from Hell.

Chapter Nine

JUST BEFORE THE BATTLE

Our trip to Hollandia was uneventful, and I was no longer worried about my ability to handle the ship. I had had quite a bit of practice before the ship was converted, and my confidence had grown. I remember the nights filled with moonlight and the calm seas. I loved to watch the sunrise and sunset. In this part of the world, they were exquisite.

The day we pulled into Hollandia was indeed a thrill. There was the largest force of ships that I had ever seen assembled in one place. There were four aircraft carriers and two battleships, but cruisers and destroyers were all over the harbor. Liberty ships, transports, LSTs, and many other types were noted. The bay was really crowded with seemingly hundreds of small boats scurrying here and there. Now we knew that we were in for something big. As our "mighty" little task force arrived, we were assigned anchorage space on the starboard side of the bay. One ship would anchor and then two others would come along each side to moor for the night.

Here I was given quite a bit of ship handling to help me become even better acquainted with the ship. Taking the ship alongside another became a habit that I thoroughly enjoyed. In approaching another ship, usually at one-third speed (six knots), I found it best to come in at an angle of about thirty degrees. I aimed the bow behind the ship that I was approaching. When I was almost on top of the ship, I would bring it about sharply until it was parallel with the other ship. When my bow was even with the other ship's conning tower, I would back down full speed, stopping all engines when the forward motion of the ship had been stopped. In the meantime, another officer had charge of the lines, and when we were close enough, he would give the orders to heave #1 (bow line), #2 (breast line), and #3 (stern line) over to the other ship. Small heaving lines were tied to the four-inch manila lines, which were passed over to the receiving ship. The lines were drawn over through receiving chocks and secured around bitts on the other ship. When all of the lines were secured, the ship, through alternating the two quads of engines, was brought closer, and slack was taken in until the ships were together. Fenders, made of manila line, were slipped between the ships to keep them at a slight distance. Then the engines were secured. If the approach was off and the stern of the ship was out too far, then the following practice was used. The port engine was set ahead at one-third speed, and the starboard quad was backed at one-third speed. The rudder was righted, usually to fifteen degrees. This would swing the stern of our ship toward the stern of the other, meanwhile taking in on the slack of #3 line. Most of the ships used four lines, but we got along with three. Anytime we went alongside another ship, I was always found on the conn, either to take it alongside or to handle the lines. This was one job I really liked to perform.

After being at Hollandia for a few days, we transferred our anchorage to a small bay behind the larger one. Here, all of the smaller craft were anchored. We found a number of our old Flotilla Five ships in here and had a number of small reunions. But our stay at Hollandia was to be quite short. We were usually going out into the larger bay to receive fuel, water, or supplies, which included one fruitless trip for rockets.

"Scuttlebutt" was flying wildly at this time. Some rumors even had us invading Japan proper. One week before we were to proceed out of Hollandia (Humboldt Bay), we received a large packet of mail that was marked "Secret." I did not notice it come aboard, nor was I told. They wanted to surprise me, and what a surprise it was. We were going to be on an invasion. We weren't going to Japan. Our destination: the Philippines by way of Leyte Island. The attack was scheduled for October 20th. We had to be ready to get underway on the 13th. It was to be a huge attack force. Many of those last seven days included a few prayers.

At this time, Van, our Skipper, received a good break. He obtained his orders to return to the good old USA. What time could be better! Poor Jim Hofmann was to take over on his release. Don

Heltzel would become Executive Officer, and I was destined to be Engineering Officer. I, who had never so much as taken a clock apart, was to become the lead "grease monkey" of the ship. Van taught me many things about the handling of the ship, and we spent many a night playing cribbage. He was a good friend. I was sorry to see him go, but I was glad for the break he had received.

On the day before we were to shove off on one of the biggest adventures that I have ever had, we loaded rockets from an LCT. We took on fifteen hundred of them. Our #2 hold contained a number of bins to house the rockets, and they were overflowing. Our last night before sailing was spent in writing many letters home, for it would be some time before we would be able to write again.

The big day dawned, and excitingly we awoke to the task before us. The convoy was not to leave until late afternoon. The morning was taken up by describing in detail to the crew what we were up against and what their respective jobs would be. We waited for seemingly endless hours before the word went around by radio to prepare to get underway. Pennants were hoisted on the halyards of the Commander's ship, and we answered by "tacking" the same signal on our halyards and running the signal to the yardarm when it was understood. Our engines were tuned, our stern winch started, and on signal, our anchor was pulled in and housed.

We were on the way to our first operation. We formed columns and returned to the larger bay, where we waited until our place in the convoy was found. We were behind the transports, toward the center. Destroyers were our screen, and they maintained the convoy in their stations and took care of "stragglers" and watched for enemy subs and planes. We had three carriers in the rear that sent up a few planes every day as scouts. We rendezvoused later with other carriers, troop ships, oilers, and supply ships. The trip to Leyte was slow, although we had good weather all the way. Our flotilla had very few breakdowns, and they were of minor nature. It was a seven-day pleasure cruise. Our excitement began to dwindle as the days passed on, and we were no longer tense. We encountered no enemy action of any kind on the way and, surprise, our greatest threat seemed to be our best weapon. The days were listless, sleepy. Sack duty was our most popular sport. Each night, we had general quarters when every man went to his battle station. This lasted for about fifteen minutes. We were in full regalia, life jackets and all. Radio silence was maintained at all times, although our small radios on the conn were used at night to inform us of any course or speed change. The crew was in good spirits, although they could not imagine, either, what lay ahead of us. We knew that on the 17th, there would be a landing of Rangers at Dinigat Island about twenty miles from Leyte. From that day on, the whole convoy would hold its "breath" for fear of being discovered. But we weren't.

On the night of the 19th, which was one of the blackest nights that I can remember, we began our trek into Leyte Gulf, passing Dinigat and newly captured Hohomohon Islands. The LSMs astern of us gave me a bad time on the mid-watch. They repeatedly crossed our stern and were out of position. Lights from Dinigat guided us through the swept channel that led to Leyte Gulf. Speed was increased. One mine was exploded, but no damage was done. I was relieved at 0400 but could not sleep, so after a cup of coffee, I went topside to watch the sun come up.

Slowly, the darkness lifted. The first gray tinge of dawn arose over the hills on our starboard side. It grew lighter. And then, from behind the hills, came a plane. It was a Jap scout plane. No ship, as yet, in the convoy was at general quarters. He circled over the convoy and dropped a bomb that landed two hundred yards off our port beam. Of all the ships in the convoy, he had to find us.

In the gray of the dawn, red tracers mixed with the white stream of firing began to fill the sky. It was a beautiful, kaleidoscopic display of fireworks. The plane was out of range by this time and was heading back to its home base. But almost every one of the ships in the convoy fired at the same time to bring him down. It filled us with awe to see the sky covered with red and white streaks against a background of gray and dirty white.

The battle for Leyte and the Philippines had begun.

Chapter Ten

THE FIGHT FOR LEYTE

A t dawn, the convoy broke up into its before-hand planned components. Leyte Gulf was like an inverted horseshoe. Our point of attack was to be in almost the exact center of the bay to the left of the capital city of Tacloban. It was near the small town of Palo. The first attack
force separated and steamed off to our port to attack the left side of the
horseshoe at the tip. This point was known as Dulag. Farther down was
another beach, which necessitated only a small force. Then on down to
the center of the "shoe" where the main forces were concentrated. These
beaches were known as "Red" and "White." Eight rocket ships were assigned to these beaches (one-half of our strength), which were almost
together, five ships to Red and three to White. As we travelled on toward
our line of departure, we were ahead of schedule, and, every once in a
while, stopped to view the proceedings. There was no AA (anti-aircraft)
fire. None was needed – yet. It seemed to be a big rehearsal.

Battleships formed a ring around the inside of the entire horseshoe. On their flanks and between them were the cruisers. The destroyers took up a position in toward the beach and divided the battleships and cruisers into sections. TRF Avengers were overhead. The
transports had stopped and anchored in the rear of the bombardment
group. Small boats were coming over their sides. LSTs and LSMs
were forming into columns to attack their landing on the various
beaches. The large LSDs (Landing Ship Dock) had disgorged their
cargo of two LCTs each. The supply ships were the farthest out for
they were not needed immediately. The troop ships had made small
circles of four transports in each group. The small boats came over
the side and were loaded when the soldiers climbed down the sides on
a rope ladder. When the boat was filled, it shoved off and the next boat

came up beside the ladder. As the boats were filled, the coxswains took them out a short way from the transport and ran in circles beside their "mother" ship.

We could see to our starboard that the two small beaches there were ready to be hit. We jockeyed forward with the four ships of our beach toward the line of departure. Everything was calm and peaceful. Things were going on as planned. 0900 was the "H" hour indicated in the Op-Plan. It was now 0800. We were ready for the pre-attack bombardment. Our rockets were loaded. We, as all the other ships had by now, taken our battle positions. No one seemed nervous. No one was afraid. We were just watching a gigantic show. There was so much to see that we did not give ourselves much thought. Then, BOOM, BOOM, the 14-inch guns went off behind us. Our ship shook, and we thought our rockets would fire. Then the cruisers opened up. The destroyers on the flanks began peppering the beach with five-inch shells. Everything seemed to be going wild all at once. The calm was shattered. The small boats filled with troops began to form columns to proceed slowly to the beach. They arrived behind us and stopped, awaiting our attack. Scout planes from the cruisers were overhead. There was no enemy fire from the beach. Then came the tension of knowing that we were in a fight. We slowly idled up to the line of departure, which was 3500 yards from our target. LCI gunboats came up on our flanks. They were to call radar ranges for us so that we could fire our rockets at the proper time. The first wave of small boats was behind us. We were ready to attack.

After forty-five minutes of shelling, the bombardment group suddenly stopped. All was silent. Now and then the staccato of 40mm gunfire from the "Cans" (destroyers) could be heard on our flanks.

Now it was our turn. The signal was given, and the attack was launched. Slowly, at six knots, we proceeded into the beach. The first wave started creeping ahead. The second wave was coming up behind them. The LSTs and LSMs began moving closer to the beach. They were loaded with troops. LCI(R)s 71, 72, 73, 74, and ourselves were advancing on Red Beach. Most of us had ducked down for cover, waiting for the rockets to be fired. My station was on the bow, and I watched the other ships attack. We were on the left flank of the five ships. All of a sudden, it happened. Mortar fire began dropping all around us. I saw the 72 get hit in the conn. The 71 was hit in the bow. Then we started firing. Salvo one, two, three, on up to twelve. I felt the ship back down full. We opened up with the 40mm and the twin 50s. I felt a sudden jar in the ship, but we went on shooting. We were turning around. The first wave of troops was going by us. I looked around toward the stern of the ship and could not see the conning tower. It was engulfed in smoke. The main deck canvas was down. Smoke was pouring out of #2 hold. Our rockets! We had been hit.

The ship was taken out of range, and all hands ran to #2 hold to see what the trouble was. Our smoke rockets had been punctured by shrapnel. Our men were running down into the hold to bring up the damaged rockets to throw over the side. It was difficult to breathe. We went back to our stations when the situation was seen to be under control.

Meanwhile, the first wave had landed, and the second was nearing the shore. The third and fourth waves were approaching rapidly. Mortar fire was still continuing. Our planes began to dive bomb interior gun emplacements. The LSTs and LSMs moved in toward the beach. LCI troop carriers moved in with them. Small control boats were moving along near the beach to hold the attacking waves in line. One could hear the steady ping, ping, whining on the beach. Sometimes a machine gun's cough could be distinguished above the steady firing. All day, ships, men, and supplies moved into the beach. A few LSTs were hit on the beach, and we were standing by to fight any fires, but we were never needed. Darkness finally overtook the landing, and all ships moved out into the safety area for the night.

Meanwhile, we made an inspection of our "wound." We had been hit with a three-inch shell through our port bulwark, and shrapnel had penetrated the deck into our rocket hold. Our smoke rockets, which covered our barrage rockets, had been punctured, and two of our barrage rockets had been scraped. We had had a close call. No other beach landing had much trouble, and of all the sixteen Rocket Ships, we had suffered eight casualties, all wounded at Red Beach. We spent the rest of the day on Condition Three. Two guns were manned, and the rest of the crew hit the sack for a much deserved rest.

Nothing happened in the next three days, although we did have "Flash Red" a number of times, indicating enemy planes in the area.,

However, only one and not more than two planes came over, primarily to scout. But October 24th brought many a tense moment, not only for us, but the entire operation.

It was early morning. We had a date with a repair ship to mend the hole in our port bulwark. Suddenly, out of the sky, came a number of planes without warning. We sounded general quarters. From the wardroom, I proceeded to my battle station. I was in the hatch by the Captain's quarters when I saw a large plane coming at us. It was on fire. I was glued to the spot. Suddenly, three hundred yards away, the plane took a quick dive and crashed into the water. As it went down, I saw two big red balls on its wing, signifying a Jap. It was a twin engine bomber. I ran to my battle station, breathing a sigh of relief, just in time to see two enemy planes crash into a tug and an LCI. The sky seemed to be raining Jap planes. We were ordered to standby to prepare to fight fires, and while we were underway, we ran over a Liberty ship's anchor cable. It put one quad of engines out of commission. So on our starboard quad, we proceeded toward the LCI after first starting for the tug. The LCI was on her side and burning badly. Men were swimming in the water. We nosed our bow up to the ship and sprayed it with our 2 1/2 –inch hoses. We finally put some fog oil on the fire, and it began to smolder. But the ship was too far gone. Slowly, silently, it turned over and disappeared. Meanwhile, other ships rescued the survivors.

We secured our hoses and steamed back forward the repair ship. We were taken alongside, and work commenced immediately. There were no more raids for a while, and we secured to Condition Three and let the repair ship (an LST) stand most of the gun watches. With our deck patched and a plate of steel on our bulwark, we limped back to our anchorage and secured. We found out that the TBFs had shot down eight planes. We claimed hits on one plane that was seen to disappear over the hills in smoke. All that day we had been tense with excitement, for the battle had really begun as far as we were concerned.

Late that afternoon, the 72 came alongside to talk over the events of the day and brought with them two monkeys, rescued from the bay. They also had a dog and wanted to give us a monkey for a pet. We kept the larger one and named it Jocko and gave the other one to the 74. The ship was now equipped with a mascot. Everyone aboard soon was bitten to prove that fact.

All that afternoon, we heard a distant rumbling over the horizon. We noticed many ships leaving the bay and returning. Scuttlebutt had it that there was a terrific sea battle going on in Surigao Straits about fifty miles south of the Gulf. This was true as we later discovered. In fact, there were three battles going on for Leyte at that moment. The Japs had surprised our forces and were attacking in three task forces. Small ships were going out to bring in survivors of the battle. Eventually, the Japs were beaten when their northern force turned and fled when they thought that Halsey was coming down from the North. The forces in the strait were beaten by the Seventh Fleet of old battleships, destroyers, and PT boats. The Japs had come within fifty miles of entering Leyte Gulf and destroying our forces accumulated there. They almost accomplished their mission. As we later learned, all large ships in the harbor were given instructions to scuttle, and the smaller ships were to go up a small strait behind Tacloban and beach to be burned. It was a close call.

The following days were filled with air raids. Sometimes one plane, sometimes more, day and night. We were at general quarters many times. It was hard to get any work done on the ship, so we spent most of our leisure time in the sack. On the 31st of October, we were warned that we were in for a storm. So we let out some anchor cable and secured everything on deck with line that was loose. There was some rain and a bit of wind that evening, but everything looked secure, and I hit the sack around ten. About one in the morning, I heard a great commotion and arose to find us in the midst of a terrific gale. The wind was really howling, and the rain was coming down so hard that it was almost impossible to see. The first thing I thought of was my life jacket, and it was the first thing I got. I went topside and could hardly hold my balance, the wind was blowing so hard. Everyone was up. I stayed in the pilot house for a while as Jim was on the conn. Don went around the ship to see if everything was okay. About 0300, when the storm began to subside a bit, we found a new menace. Seven large 15 x 100 foot Army barges were headed for our stern. We slacked off on our anchor cable, but to no avail. Three of the barges went by after bumping the ship a bit. By this time, we were "dragging anchor." Our engines had been running all night. The fourth barge snapped our anchor cable as if it were string, and we had lost an anchor. For the rest of the night, we had to get underway. We sailed out toward the mouth of the bay and then returned. By that time, it was morning, and the storm had all but subsided.

We sent out an emergency message that we were without an anchor and had only one quad of engines working. The 73 had a spare anchor, so we proceeded to her vicinity to claim it. I took it as close to the 73 as I dared in the rough sea, while Don and Jim had the boatswain's mate tab on a messenger line to heave to the other ship. The other end of the heaving line was tied to our anchor cable. The line was then attached to the spare anchor, and I pulled our ship ahead. The anchor came off the bow of the 73. We pulled it in with the stern winch to 30 fathoms and sat for the rest of the day.

The next few weeks brought a few tense moments, including many air raids on the second Sunday that found us at general quarters for a period of thirty-six hours. Here, while aiding a disabled LCI on the beach, we were strafed by a Jap "Val" (a small fighter plane) and suffered our first casualty. Our radioman was hit in the hand. The same "Val" strafed a gasoline dump and set it afire. We went down the beach to fight it. However, with our one quad, we were told to lay off the beach and be used as a supply ship for the others. I went ashore for the second fire with Fire Party #2 and had quite a time. The water was up to our necks when we went over the bow, and we had to swim a bit for shallow water. We passed the hoses through and started the pumps and sprayed our quarry of burning trucks. The fire was almost out, and some of us were returning to the ship to pass the word that the water could be turned off when a spray of bullets spattered around us. Everyone ducked, and I lost my watch in the water. We scurried up the ladder and pulled our equipment aboard and "high-tailed" it out of there. The 72, on our port side, had the same idea and pulled out at the same time. In the dark, with our one quad giving us a bad time, we had a minor collision that injured one man. Then we had to go around the bay hunting for a doctor. Another LCI came up alongside to transfer the man and gave us one of the best examples of ship handling that I had ever seen. It was pitch dark, and we were afloat. But the other Skipper came around our stern and glided up alongside, backed down full, stopped, we made the transfer, and he pulled away. It was done in three minutes.

We had one big air raid in November that we missed. One Sunday, we were called to Dulag to fight fires, and our one quad didn't make the ten miles in any hurry. We pulled up at Dulag to find the fires under control and the attacking planes hitting the shipping at Tacloban. So we turned around and returned to base. By the time we got there, the planes had gone, but fires were still smoldering. One LST repair ship was hit by a suicide plane, and from the report by the 338, it was a mess. Many men were trapped by the crashing plane, and one section of the ship was a mass of arms, legs, and blood.

That was the last big air raid the Japs held over Leyte.

On the same day, Ensign Charlie Gaskins reported aboard. He was our new fourth officer. He came aboard in the middle of the air raid. I welcomed him, and one of the men handed him a battle helmet and a life jacket. He was on his own. But finally, the raid was over, and the ship secured to calmer waters and anchored. We got acquainted with our new officer and found out that he was from Indiana. We then filled him with our stories of our duty. Scuttlebutt now had it that we were in for another operation. Poor Charlie moaned. He had come aboard at the wrong time. He was out of the States three weeks. I was now an "old salt" of eight months.

We lost our cook at this time. He was transferred to a hospital ship with a stomach disorder.

The next two weeks were peaceful in comparison with the past month. We were not veterans, but we didn't feel like it. We were soon to learn that with all of the supplies coming aboard and having our bad quad fixed on Thanksgiving on an LSD, was going to bring us more action.

Our biggest fight was over, and it was a rough one. Our next one was also going to prove very interesting as we were destined to enter the Japs' back door.

My Log

November 9, 1944

Dear Mother and Dad:
Yesterday was a hard day. First we heard of F.D.R.'s 4th term and on top of that we had another storm. They are quite frequent up here and they are not very <u>nice</u>. In fact, there it is, 24 hours later and still blowing although to a lesser degree. Before I continue, I want to say, don't worry about me for we are just sitting while the Air Force goes to war. We'll be sitting here for quite a while yet.

So you want to be a sailor, Dad? These are the first storms I have ever witnessed and I was scared to death at the first one for it happened at night and I came topside and could see nothing but a swirling sea amidst rain and a 70 mile gale. The one last night couldn't make up its mind so it blew from two directions. To hold a ship at anchor in the bay, you have two helpers and one assistant. By that I mean you have (1) an anchor, (2) power, and the assistant, the rudder. Around midnight the anchor began to drag, in other words, the wind and sea were so strong that they took the ship for an involuntary jaunt. When a ship drags anchor, you do not have much you can do to control her movements. As we only had four engines instead of eight engines only. The only thing we could do was to back, hoping we wouldn't get the anchor cable caught in our good propeller. We bring in the anchor by a motor driven winch and it is in the open on the stern. And you know that any motor caught in the rain is very stubborn about starting. Also, when you back down on one quad of engines, (the propeller will turn counter-0clockwise) taking you to the opposite side of the working quad. Influence here is the amount of current and the position of the stern anchor and tending cable. So you see there are quite a few things to be taken into account. It shouldn't have been so bad but we drifted down on an L57 and after a half hour of frantic work we got the stern winch started and began pulling in the anchor and backing at the same time. It was close. We brought in the anchor and backed into a new anchorage where we sit this morning rocking with the sea. I didn't get to bed until 4:30 in the morning.

Such is an unusual day at sea.
So now, the people can get back to the war and get the damn thing over with. I hope the people are getting tired of war back there, for when they do, they will want prompt action.

E. F. Sheeran

So another day is ending. In 2 weeks I'll have 9 months overseas. Half-over. Slow but sure. So say a prayer for me and have faith for I'll be home someday, looking forward to a quart of fresh milk and a sirloin steak mixed with

    Love to all, Eddie.

Chapter Eleven

ORMOC

The land battle, by this time, had carried across the island, but had bogged down in the mud, which came in December and seemed to last forever. True, also, we still had only one air field on Leyte for two others had sunk in swamps. The Japs were reinforcing their troops on the other side of the island by bringing them in from the sea. The situation was getting quite serious and a meeting of the "big chiefs" brought rumors that new plans were being made. Although the new operation was a big secret, we soon found out about it. Soon the Op-Plan came aboard and we discovered that a small force of the 77th Division was going to circle Leyte and land on the other side to surprise and surround the Japs. Four rocket ships were slated for this operation which was almost entirely amphibious. Destroyers were our screen, APD's, our large troop carriers, LST's, LSM's, and LCI's made up the rest of the supply and troop carrying ships. The attack was set for dawn on December 7, 1944.

We left Leyte Gulf at 1300 on the 6th to form up and maintain convoy positions. On board for the operation was War Correspondent Jack Dowling of the *Chicago Sun*. Our trip would take us through the Suragao Straits around the bottom of Leyte and up its other side to Ormoc Bay. The trip was short, but speed was slow. Our ETA (Estimated Time of Arrival) must be just before dawn to use the weapon of surprise. The trip was made in calm water, but the night was very black, and we guided on the ship ahead by watching its wake, the small phosphorescent glow of the ship. Just as it was getting light, we sailed into Ormoc Bay, and, on the signal "Deploy," sailed ahead of the larger ships that had led the way. We jockeyed into our positions on the line of departure. Our ship was on the right flank. The crew was just beginning to get comfortable in their battle stations, when out of the sky sped a plane and headed for the beach. It was just light enough to see him. Almost all of the ships opened up on him before it was realized that it was a P-40, which resembles a Jap "Zero." Unfortunately, the plane was hit, but not downed, and the plane flew away. It wasn't supposed to be there, and he gave us a scare. The convoy returned it.

At H-Hour minus 15 minutes, we started our attack. Rocket after rocket was fired until the load was exhausted, and then we fired our automatic weapons at the beach. There was no return fire. The little three-knot sea-going tanks began to pass us on the way to the beach, and they were filled with soldiers. Some were laughing, some were glum, but they all waved a greeting as they passed. We felt a lump of sympathy for them. We turned about and traveled from the beach and dropped our anchor to view the invasion. I brought my camera on the bow to snap some pictures.

While we were sitting around, there was a sudden rumble near the tip of the bay. A plane was sighted, then another. They were Japs. Then we saw our P-38s arriving. There were dogfights. The Japs tried to unload their bombs. One enemy plane was downed by a P-38. But another headed for a destroyer. WHAM! It went right into the side of the "Can," but the damage did not seem to be serious. We began to form into convoy positions to escape the air raids. Now we learned that there was a Jap reinforcement attack around the island made up of eleven ships. Our outer screen of destroyers had engaged them, with the aid of the P-38s. That left us without cover. So the Jap planes attacked us. It was almost a survival test. Fortunately, we had the largest force, but Jap planes kept showing up, out of nowhere. We went to general quarters. We secured from general quarters. We went. We secured. That went on throughout the day. The convoy was steaming rapidly out of the bay when another air attack found us. We stood in horror watching a Jap plane dive straight for a destroyer. A P-38 was trying to bring him down. But the Jap made it. Straight into the bridge he dove, and the destroyer was immediately covered from bow to stern with a huge mass of flames. It was sickening. Then another enemy plane was sweeping over the convoy and, being one of the first ships in the columns, we waited for him, and when he was zooming by, all our guns opened up on him, and he crashed into the sea about four hundred yards ahead of our flagship. Another plane was coming around our stern, and the 40mm fired eight shots at him, and he was winged. The 20mm's on the stern put more punctures in him, and his apparent destination, an APD, was interrupted. We had knocked down two planes in five minutes. There were more raids through the rest of the day, but most were aimed at our destroyer screen. Around 1800 hours, it began to grow far, and we saw storm clouds on the horizon. For once, we were glad to see them, for with a storm over our heads, we were safer than ever from an air raid. We were still afraid of a midget sub attack.

The darkness that ensued brought minor havoc to the convoy as the blackness broke up the column a bit. We were the guide ship in the right hand column, and when I took the morning watch, we were the only ship in the column. The rest of the ships were all over the place. Some were following the APD on our starboard. Others had shifted into the next column. But our Commander signaled that all ships should return to Leyte any way possible. We had left two LSMs and one LCI on the beach at Ormoc. They returned the next day, unharmed. We pulled into Leyte Gulf very much relieved. We were not surprised to find that they had had a large air raid the night before. We watched as the ships in our convoy passed by our anchorage and counted their wounds. There were many. We had had a total of twenty-one separate air raids and twenty-seven Jap planes had been shot down. Later, we discovered that we lost five P-38s, but all of the pilots were rescued. It had been a successful operation. There were some casualties, but fewer than expected. Most of the casualties occurred on the destroyer that had been hit by a suicide plane.

We were glad to return since Christmas was coming, and we were getting anxious about our mail and packages. Sometimes our mail would arrive after nine or ten days from the States, and at other times, it would take two months and even more. At this time, the mail was coming in rather slow due to the lack of mailmen overseas and the load that comes with Christmas. On December 24th, we received ten big turkeys, and we had a feast that night and all on Christmas Day. We had a quiet Christmas, although one Jap plane came over to extend his greetings. For New Year's, we found a ship that was having beer problems and bought five cases from them. Each member of our crew had three bottles apiece. That was our New Year's Eve celebration.

On the 17th of December, we had watched a convoy of ships pull out for another operation. This force was to land at Mindoro, just below Luzon. Even with that force leaving, more and more ships began to arrive until our suspicions became aroused. On New Year's Day, we received another Op-Plan, which was really thick. It was to be the biggest invasion in this area. Luzon was the location, but not the southern part that housed the modern port of Manila. It was to land at Lingayen Gulf in northern Luzon and work down from there.

We passed the days preparing for the long journey by overhauling one engine and working on the launchers. Our #2 hold was filled with rockets, and we had plenty of ammunition aboard. But food was scarce, especially fresh meat and vegetables. We had quite a time with supplies. The men on the ship were beginning to show, slightly, the effects of battle. There was little or no liberty for Tacloban was not a large city. However, we made the mail trip once in a while, just to give a few men a chance to stretch their legs. The change did not last too long. There was no interest in Tacloban. However, it was some reminder of home, although the buildings were ramshackle, and only one really modern building was in the town. But once in a while, we saw a Coca-Cola sign, or a barber shop, or a fruit stand, and a small restaurant that was our first glimpse of "civilization" in some time. We gladly retired to the ship to spend our leisure. With sighing resignation, we made ready for our new trip and operation, expecting quite a battle for positions that far north.

The invasion was scheduled for January 9th, and we left Leyte on January 3rd, with the biggest convoy I have ever seen.

My Log

December 3, 1944

Dad, I hope this to be one of those man to man talks. I haven't written to you in this way for quite some time and I believe it to be past time.

First of all I want to answer some of your questions. You are quite correct on where I received the letter. Yes, we were in on the first wave and hit the toughest beach but came out of it with hardly any excitement. You can see by now that you are right on the meaning of the "G." It should really be an "R" but we are designated as a gunboat. I have received the headspace that you sent me and I believe that I have informed you by this time but for security's sake will repeat.

Dad, I know how mother worries and I believe that it would have been smarter for me not to tell her where I am. But it was so unusual for me that I couldn't help it. Yes, it was fairly tough going into the beach but fear was forgotten; everything happened so fast. We did a swell job and God was with us for a couple of fellows were very lucky.

Dad, I hate to become solemn, but someday I have to with someone pointing out the possibilities that may come to pass. There is no one else but you. A father seems to understand the situation of his son far better than anyone else, naturally. On an operation of this kind, things are pretty well taken care of by the time we go into the beach but there is always a possibility that they missed something, and this time they did. It isn't the beachhead that we became afraid of, it was the aftermath, the air-raids, and there were a number of them, small but tough. There is not much rest for there is always a tension, a tightness, that can't seem to be conquered. You probably recognized the factors when you proposed to mother. But this one lasts for weeks. However, that has seemingly all passed, but we are not too sure. Don't believe that the war is over by a long shot. True, this may become the climax of the war for there is more happening here than meets the eye. It is still a good fight. We have been hampered by Mother Nature.

Dad, if anything should ever happen to me and there is a chance, considering where I am, I want you to help me in the distribution of my wealth. Dad, I know that this sounds morbid, but I am taking no chances, for one never knows. However, no matter where you are there is always the possibility of accident. I want to ask your advice

54

*on some of the small things that need straightening out. As you know now, Peg and I want to become engaged at the earliest possible moment and I must think of her in some way. [*What he meant was making the engagement official and public.*] What would you advise? It doesn't have to be a great deal as you know. You are the beneficiaries of all my wealth, but I was thinking that of all the happiness she has brought me I could sign over my bonds to her, only in case of accident however. Dad, I know that we very seldom go into an operation and when we do, it lasts for only a short space of time. There is always the chance of a lucky hit and that is what we would have to receive for we are no target for anyone.*

Dad, I believe that I have made myself clear in some respect and sincerely ask your advice.

*Turning to the lighter side, what do you think of the idea of proposing for me? Not that I want anyone to take my place, but it seems to be the best substitute that we can think of. I hope you receive it as an honor for we meant it in that way. Announcement of the engagement would necessarily follow for I am certain and I believe that you like her very much. Let me know as soon as possible for I would like to buy it [*the ring*] for her birthday. [*April 8*]*

Well, dad, I believe that this is the end of the message that I wanted you to have. I hope that you are getting settled and not working too hard. Tell Mr. Dewey I would like very much to re-capture his son.

Before I close, I want to advise, keep your eyes to the map and your ears to the radio concerning this area. We are becoming very important.

     Love,
     Ed
Ensign E.F. Sheeran
O.S.S. LCI (G) 331-Flot 7
c/o F.P.O. San Francisco, Calif.

    Mr. E.P. Sheeran
    Dayton, Ohio
c/o Frigidaire Corp. – Main Office

[Edward Patrick Sheeran, General Manager of Frigidaire in Dayton, was a self-educated second-generation Irish guy. He went to school through the eighth grade, and then he went to work to support his family.

55

He continued his education, however, in night classes. I'm not sure how he met Mary Elizabeth McDonald, who lived in a big white house with pillars in Dayton, but he must have charmed her mightily. But he won her over, and they had three children, Donald, Lillian, and Eddie (both Don and Eddie also went by "Pat," and Grandpa was called "Pat." I don't know how the family managed with that, maybe it was the tone of voice.)

Upon receipt of Dad's letter about proposing to Peg, Grandpa did as asked. He did buy a diamond ring and he drove to South Bend, where Peggy was finishing her senior year at Saint Mary's. He took her to dinner, and then, back at Saint Mary's, he dropped to his knee and offered her the ring. And, as the story goes, since he was studying Spanish at night just then, my-Irish-up-by-his-bootstraps-charming-painter- on-the-side-grandfather proposed in Spanish to my ten-years-from-then-mother-German-major on behalf of his son, off in the South Pacific with Japanese war planes dropping bombs on him.

She said yes.

And both held hands and hoped that Eddie would get home safe and sound -- and soon.]

Chapter Twelve

THE INVASION OF LUZON

This convoy, larger than the one that sailed for Leyte, was formed in the usual manner. The large transports were first, then the amphibious craft, including LSTs, LSMs, LSDs, and LCIs. Four Destroyers and two Cruisers were our screen, and we had a number of Destroyer Escorts along. Carriers brought up the rear. Three days prior to the landing would be a scheduled bombardment from Battleships, Cruisers, Destroyers, and LCI Gunboats of the Seventh Fleet. Minesweeping would take place at the same time and continue for three days. Our trip took us below Leyte and into the Suragao Straits above Mindanao. We would pass Cebu, Negros, and Panay on our starboard. Then turning northward, we would pass Mindoro and the Verde Island passage separating it from Luzon. Then, still northward, passing Manila Bay and on one hundred miles to the mouth of Lingayen Gulf. It was quite a long trip and it was very slow.

We had more excitement on this trip than the one to Leyte. The sea was calm up to Mindoro and the nights delightfully filled with moonlight. On the 7th, we had a couple of air raids, but they were against the second section of the convoy. The whole task force was divided into two large components. On the night of the 8th, while I had the watch, there was a sudden flare to our starboard. Then, a flash of gunfire. Instantly, it seemed that everyone was up on deck. It was a night battle of destroyers. We were passing Manila Bay in the dead of night, but some enemy destroyers had lurked there and had attacked our screen. Our ships were sending up flare after flare and finally sighted the enemy. Two "Nip" destroyers were sunk, and anything else Japanese afloat, fled. Our task force passed on amid congratulations to our screen for destroying the enemy so capably.

We hit Lingayan Gulf at midnight on the 8th. It was very rough going into the huge bay. It was almost twenty miles to our attacking positions. We were sailing slowly into the bay when all of a sudden, I saw a huge round object ahead of us. Immediately, I swerved the ship to avoid it, and the ships behind followed suit. Word was passed that a probable mine was in the center of the convoy. No explosion was reported.

We proceeded toward our objective with dawn overtaking us. At dawn, the force was broken up, and the transports formed small circles in a larger circle. Boats were coming over their sides before they had dropped anchors. The battleships and cruisers had lined up about three miles from the beach to throw in their welcome to Lingayen. They made up the huge inner support ring. There were five main beach areas altogether. We were in the third, or middle one, but not much resistance was expected from our part of the bay. Our objective was a small town called San Fabian. Four Rocket Ships, the 73, 74, 341, and ourselves had been picked for White Beach One. Eight Rocket Ships were farther down to our port. Four were to our starboard on Blue Beach. The ammo, supply, and miscellaneous craft were farther out in the bay behind the transport area. As we were proceeding toward our line of departure, a lone Jap plane came over, and the sky was soon filled with "ack-ack." But he was out of range.

Our final position was marked by a patrol craft and two sub chasers. Of the four rocket ships in our section, we were second from the right with the 341 on our starboard. Again we found ourselves in line, ready for battle. The "big stuff" opened up, and we watched the bombardment of the beaches. Instead of waiting for the end of the bombardment, we were to proceed with the first wave of LVPs (small, light sea-going tanks carrying about 25 men each) into the beach. The run was going to take thirty minutes because of the slow speed of the LVPs. We had one quad ahead at one-third speed. We fired twenty-two rockets every fifty seconds. Those interval seconds were like hours. On the bow, we thought up something new. Since there was so much time between salvoes, we were going to use the 40mm to strafe the beach on the way in. We fired eight rounds between rocket blasts and then hugged the deck until the next round was fired.

On the approach, one of our cruisers fired too short, and it landed in front of the 341. This bothered the 341, so they called and informed us that they were moving over. They had slowed down in the meantime, and when they finally did come over, they were quite a ways behind us. But they still fired their rockets. Some of those rockets landed about one hundred yards in front of our bow. Then we got sore. The 341 stopped shooting. On and on the time dragged until after a seemingly endless eternity, we backed down and watched the landing after we had strafed the beach. Our four ships retreated to a small anchorage away from the beach and out of the way of the landing waves. Sitting there, watching the proceedings, we suddenly heard a loud roar and saw to our startled eyes that the 341 had discharged another round of rockets. They were headed straight for the battleship West Virginia. But they didn't reach that far. They fell short, fortunately, the West Virginia was the only target around. After that exhibition, the 341 lapsed into a conversational coma for some time. But meanwhile, the landing was going on as it had been planned. Wave after wave of troops hit the beach. One of the small boats was hit, and we saw all the men scramble out safely and advance into the beach on foot.

We were looking through our binoculars at the beach when one of the signalmen spotted our approach to the beach and excitedly reported that we had knocked out a pillbox. And there, on the beach, was a fortification that our 40mm had peppered with 350 rounds. It was in a shambles. But the shock came when we saw two planes hidden behind the trees that we had also hit. What planes were doing there no one will probably ever know. Naturally, we wanted to paint all of our war "victims" on the side of the conn. During the entire landing, there was little return fire from the beach and no opposition from the air. All day, troops and supplies moved into the beach and MacArthur waded ashore again.

In the afternoon, we were loafing around with Condition Three set with Charlie on the conn, when over the cruiser Australia, flying low, came a Jap "Zero." It was headed right at us and could have strafed the whole ship, but he was either out of ammunition or he didn't want to waste his ammo on such a small target. Everybody ducked, including Charlie on the conn where he found refuge under the small radio, bumping heads with the signalman. That had been a close call, for many of the men had been outside, and he could not have missed everyone. We took a few pot shots at him, but he was soon out of sight.

In the three days that we stayed at Lingayen, there were only a few Jap planes sighted, and they were either shot down or they were out of range to start with. At night, our air force sent over some P-61s, which were built on the order of P-38s, with the same twin tail assembly. Some "trigger happy" ship started shooting at the first one, and everyone joined in. The P-61s retired and didn't return.

Standing by one afternoon near our designated rocket flagship, we received a blinker message from a large AKA off of our stern. The message asked us to investigate an object floating in the water near our ship. We searched and were grimaced with horror as our eyes located a body bobbing with the incoming tide. We transferred the message to our flagship, who relayed it to the shore station. A small boat was sent out to pick up the body. It was an American sailor. I shall never forget his outstretched arms reaching toward heaven.

We were scheduled to leave with the rest of our group on the fourth day but had fuel pump trouble and had to hunt up a repair ship to get fixed up and left the next day with another returning convoy. It was one of the roughest trips that we ever encountered. One "swell" almost turned the wardroom upside down, with dishes and chairs flying every way. We had run into the edge of a typhoon. We finally arrived at Mindoro and retraced our steps through the straits to Leyte Gulf and Tacloban and mail. It was now the middle of January, and we were destined for a short rest.

Air raids on Leyte had almost ceased as we now had air superiority over the Philippines.

Chapter Thirteen

BACK TO LUZON

In January, we spent some leisure time re-exploring our liberty port of Tacloban, the capital of Leyte. It was located near the waterfront. A huge Army dock, entirely surrounded by mud, took up most of this space. Behind the waterfront lay the city proper. Tacloban had suffered. Many of the one-story buildings had been hit by repeated air raids from both sides. The city was situated on a peninsula with the air strip at its tip. A small bay lay on one side and larger Leyte Gulf on the other. The streets were uniform, and curbs separated the sidewalks of dirt from the jeep-traveled highways. The business section of about three blocks consisted of all one-story structures. There was a barber shop operated by women, a restaurant that would be snubbed by American tramps, a drug store, a fruit stand, souvenir stands, and a small clothing store. They were all open in front with the merchandise scattered over the entire interior. There was no organization. However, there was precious little to sell. Don and I, ashore for the day, walked through the "downtown" section to the residential palaces. One-story frame homes of no more than two rooms each housed our liberated. Most houses were built on stilts to keep out insects and water. Thatched roofs gave some protection from the elements, the worst being the sun. Little tots roamed the streets, begging for a penny or a smoke. Older people shuffled away the day with seemingly nothing to do. Women, dark and dirty, sat on the steps of their homes waiting for something to happen. Army trucks roamed everywhere. Jeeps were always in the way. The streets were muddy, and dirt gutters were filled with water.

After an hour's jaunt, the sights seemed to become more sickening, so we decided to return to the ship and stay out of the mud. We were afraid to eat or drink anything in the town.

In between these vey occasional trips to the "city," we loafed and toiled aboard ship trying to keep her in shape for the next operation. We could see no end to the fighting. We consistently worked on the launchers and engines to keep them ready for any eventuality. We were still receiving Christmas mail and sometimes books came aboard to entertain our eyes. LCIs came into the area loaded with rockets, and we all groaned. Later, these rockets were distributed along with another "secret" mail delivery. Another operation was in the wind. Commander Day was in charge of this one, and as far as planning and organization, it was the best. We got everything we wanted in supplies and needs. Any ship that came into the area was scrutinized by the Commander for food and clothing. However, the fresh meat situation remained grave, and very little was found. This was the beginning of the second month on Spam and corned beef rations.

We were briefed on the purpose and facts of the operation and found it was to be a reconnaissance only. We were to land units of the 11th Airborne Division behind the Jap lines at Nasugbu, Luzon. Nasugbu was located eighteen miles south of Manila Bay, and this force was a feint against the southern flank of the Jap lines. This, again, was a complete amphibious operation. Destroyers were our largest units, and there were precious few of them. Four Rocket ships, eight LSTs, four LCI Gunboats, four DEs (Destroyer escorts), four DDs, four LSMs, and six LCI troop carriers made up the entire task force. It was small, indeed, in comparison with the force that landed at Leyte and Lingayen that had, approximately, fourteen hundred ships in each. However, two days previous, there was to be a landing at Subic Bay, Luzon, forty miles above Manila that took a somewhat larger force in that vicinity. It was a double thrust at Manila.

We were scheduled to leave on the afternoon of January 26th to land on the morning of the 29th. We filled up with fuel, water, and supplies and waited for the eventful day. We were working the crew eight hours each day for the principle reason that boredom and monotony were becoming our greatest "enemies." The four of us would spend the day supervising with intervals of coffee drinking and "bull slinging." Our biggest recreation was reading.

The day arrived, and we prepared to get underway. Our Task Force proceeded first to Tolosa in Leyte Gulf to rendezvous with other components of the unit and then proceeded out of the bay and around the well-known route of Suragao Straits, passing around Panay and heading northward along the shores of Mindaro, passing the rough Verde Island passage and to the southern part of Luzon. We encountered no air action but had quite a surprise from undersea craft. Passing Panay, just above Mindanao during daylight hours, we were interrupted by a loud explosion on the port side of the convoy. A puff of black smoke arose from one of the screening destroyers, and she veered out of the column. She had been torpedoed. The rest of the screen closed in tighter around the convoy, and two "cans" were dispatched to contact the attacking sub. No contact was made, and the sub escaped to its base, which was in all probability the port of Cebu City, where it was known that a midget sub base was still in operation against our forces. Meanwhile, the destroyer was floundering in the sea and reported that her engine room had been hit and put out of action. She was taken in tow by another destroyer and brought up the rear of the convoy. This had happened on the first day out, and the entire convoy became "safety" conscious the remaining two. No further action developed, and the disabled destroyer was left at Mindoro. We proceeded at dawn on the 29th into the small indentation in the island of Luzon, called Nasugbu. We took our place on the line of departure, which was only 2000 yards from the beach and watched the LSTs unload their troops in LCVPs. The LSM and LCI troop carriers awaited closely behind. The destroyers were on the flanks and began popping away at targets of opportunity almost immediately. The 5-inch guns of the destroyers seemed like "pop guns" in comparison with the heavy guns of the battleships. We had an eight-plane coverage.

The signal was given, and again we were going into a hostile beach. Salvo number one was fired, and from our position on the left flank, we could see that they were taking effect on the beach. Numerous puffs of smoke arose on the shore, and after four salvoes, the beach was obscured. We finished our twelfth and strafed with our 40 mm until the boats had passed us and were closing in on the beach. By the time our rocket barrage was completed, we were a scant four hundred yards from the beach. The first wave hit the sandy shore, and the second and third were due from the LSMs and LCIs. Commander Day, aboard the 73, located a Jap machine gun nest in a barn close to the beach and went in to "pepper" it with 40 mm fire. A destroyer on our left flank had the same idea and slowly backed down into position, stopped, fired one burst, and the side of the barn disappeared in a puff of smoke. The machine gun was not heard from after that.

This landing was to have been a reconnaissance only, but it went so well that it was followed through as a small invasion. There were only two casualties all day, and they were Army, wounded by snipers. D-Day afternoon found us observing a parade of natives on the sands waving American and Philippine flags.

We were to have pulled out for Mindoro the same day, but the LSTs were stranded on the beach and could not get off until high tide the next morning. The screen and LCI gunboats and rocket ships formed outer and inner screens around the beach protecting the LSTs. We had an attack of Japanese Q-boats that night. A Q-boat is a small 25-footer, usually loaded with TNT of gasoline and was used in suicide tactics. The next day, the LSTs still could not get off the beach, and we had to wait for another day before they were finally freed. Thankfully, we returned to Mindoro. From Mindoro, we made the trip to Leyte again with a small convoy and returned to our old anchorage in Leyte Gulf.

February was spent in peace and following the news broadcasts that were beginning to sound brighter with each passing day. Manila had been liberated.

The Philippines were almost ours again. However, there were a few more Jap held spots we hadn't thought of, that someone else did. Air raids on Leyte had ceased, and it was now a huge port loaded with shipping.

Chapter Fourteen

PUERTO PRINCESA, PALAWAN

The middle of February brought with it another Op-Plan, and we were disappointingly curious to see where we were now heading. To us, it seemed that we had run out of places to invade. But this new, rather small invasion was going to take us southwest of Leyte instead of to the heart of Japan. We were going to storm Puerto Princesa, Palawan. Palawan is a long thin island almost directly west of Panay Island. The operation was going to be staged from Mindoro. With a week to go, we prepared to get underway to follow our familiar route through the straits and up the islands to Mindoro. The route was beginning to be so familiar that at time the helmsman practically took over the ship. Night watches began to get boring because of the lack of action which no one, naturally, wanted and the day watches began to become quite warm. We rigged up a small canvas over the conn for this emergency.

The trip to Mindoro proved uneventful, and we arrived to find that we were the last to report, and we pulled into the beach for a few days' rest. There wasn't much to do on the Mindoro beach, and most of the time was spent aboard ship. The beach was sandy, and the "bay," which housed the task force, was not a bay at all. It was a small indentation in the land that afforded little protection against the elements. There was a small bay to the starboard upon entering, but it was very shallow and could house only a few ships. The terrain of Mindoro was flat but gradually raised until small hills could be seen in the far mist-covered interior. Coconut palms were not so common here, and it seemed to give us an entirely new setting. The background of the beach was drab with a curtain of dust. The small interior of San Jose supplied a bit of liberty for the crew in the few days that followed.

At this time, we were having a bit of trouble with the engines and overhauled one in a day, which is quite an accomplishment in itself. We were ready to furnish fire power for our sixth operation. This was the sixth to our credit because we had found out that we had been given Wakde, New Guinea to our list of invasions, although we had not arrived until two weeks after the operation had taken place.

The task force invading Palawan was made up of two Cruisers and a number of Destroyers, while two Aircraft Carriers tarried in the background. It was another amphibious operation but was quite large. There were nine small transports, and the remainder was made up of LSTs, LSMs, and LCIs. There were only four rocket ships assigned the detail of "beach cleaning," the 224, 230, 341, and ourselves. We left Mindoro on the afternoon of the 26th and would arrive at Puerto Princesa on the dawning of the 28th. The journey to Panay was without excitement, but once we had made our turn westward that would take us toward Palawan, we encountered some decidedly rough water. This was the famous Sulu Sea, fed from the north by the China Sea through the narrow straits between Mindoro and a group of small islands. The swells pounded us relentlessly throughout the night, and when we made our last change of course, slightly southward, it took us directly into the "trough" and tossed us like a shell on the sea. Another wardroom calamity occurred that tossed Don clear off his bunk and gave the dishes the look of a new bride's kitchen. The steady rolling from side to side introduced slight sleepiness with its lullaby rhythm. Don joined me on the conn because he couldn't stay in bed.

The night passed slowly. Dawn silently stole over the convoy. Ahead was our objective. At first glimpse, it was very small. The bay was an inverted "V", and, as we approached, we saw that it was indeed narrow. Our objective was on the right near the tip. According to the various charts, the bay was very shallow. Opposition was reported as minor before we had even sailed. This meant that there was a small garrison left by the Japs to protect the harbor.

We had also heard that one hundred fifty American prisoners had been slaughtered by the Japs on Christmas Day of 1944. General MacArthur had passed on the order to our troops that no Japanese prisoner was to be taken.

Our line of departure, due to the small restricted bay, was to be a scant one thousand yards and was bordered by trees and jungle growth so thick that we could not comprehend how our troops were to penetrate it. We idled up to our position, affixed beforehand by Commander Day's instructions. Then we waited. Admiral Barbey on the Spencer was directly behind us. The small transports and amphibious craft anchored in the middle of the bay and began to load their boats. Out of the huge cavernous mouths of the LSTs rolled the small, light, sea-going tanks filled with eight men each. Our air cover of four P-61s droned overhead.

As the first wave slowed at our stern, we waited for the signal to attack. It came, and immediately we fired number one salvo and began to slowly edge to the beach. But something was wrong. Looking back to the conn, because the rockets had not fired again, we saw the Skipper and Don frantically waving their arms to fire on the beach. The 40mm began to pump lead as we on the bow could not begin to imagine what had happened. The 40mm could not fire too long for the advancing waves had already passed our bow. We were greeted with hoots from the boys in the tanks and probably deserved them, for we had offered our troops little protection. We retired upstream and anchored, while the waves of troops beached, one after the other. All hands' attention was turned to the conn to find out the trouble, but there was no solution. The rockets had refused to be fired. The first round had fired O.K., but the rest had not gone off. We checked the entire system, finally blaming it on faulty electrical wiring. The electrician was called, but he could not offer any answer. Tempers began to fly, and the electrician ended up with a month restriction. However, neither the Admiral nor Commander noticed that we had had a rather large misfire, and nothing was said. However, it had to go on our report. We relaxed to watch the proceedings.

As our troops moved in, the Filipinos moved out. Some came out in canoes, and a few came aboard our ship. We were instructed to bring them to the U.S.S. Spencer (the Admiral's flagship) for questioning. The slaughter of the American prisoners was upheld in their statements. We then proceeded to a small group of islands in the bay to return the natives to their homes. Being on the conn and taking the ship with the assistance of a native guide, the ship was run embarrassingly on a sandbar. We were stuck there for the evening and had to await high tide at midnight that loosened the bottom enough to retract. The operation in itself was a success as there was no return fire from the beach and very little opposition in the interior. The Japs had fled to the hills. There were no prisoners taken.

Our stay at Puerto Princesa was involved with the duty of guarding the harbor entrance. The day after the invasion, we sent a few men ashore to get a glimpse of the island. They returned with a few souvenirs, including parts of enemy planes. However, they were a bit disturbed when the fact came out that the island was still mined, especially around the airfield, where they had been.

Two days later, we got underway to return to Mindoro. The convoy wasn't too large, and the greater part of it was going to Leyte. On the second night, the larger component parted, and the four rocket ships and one minesweeper turned toward Mindoro. We returned to the daily flow of life aboard as liberty was almost taboo because of the disinterest for the island.

However, we had only been there a few days when we received new orders to return to Leyte. The convoy included only the 224 and ourselves, so it was decided that we were to proceed through the inner straits, which an LCI could navigate and make the trip in thirty-seven hours, compared with the four-day trip otherwise. The straits led below Mindoro, east above Panay and Negros, southeast passing the small island of Masbate and Samar into the upper part of Leyte. Here we came into contact with the San Juanico Straits that wound southward through the separating pass between Samar and Leyte and thence into Leyte Gulf. The trip took a little longer than one day, and we began our trek in the afternoon, which would give us ample room at night in the larger inner sea. Dawn of the next morning would find us near Masbate, and we would make Leyte in the early evening of the next day.

The trip through the San Juanico Straits wound here and there, and was one of decided interest. Everywhere, the natives came out in their canoes and greeted us. We were cheered roundly by every village along the shore as we passed. The surroundings were quite beautiful. It was an intermingling of light and dark green, stirred with the rays of the sun that gave it a perfect tropical setting. We traveled through the straits at a speed of ten knots, which was rather precarious, but we were happy enough to get away from the front and felt that we were on our way to a well-deserved rest.

We were wrong.

Chapter Fifteen

PANAY AND NEGROS

Leyte Gulf and the small bay around Tacloban were crowded with shipping. Upon entering, we encountered many of our old Flotilla Five ships now assigned to new duties. Some were salvage ships, and others received the very excellent task of spare parts ships. This included trips from Leyte to Manus Island in the Admiralty's near New Guinea, hauling parts to the repair bases.

We pulled into the pier at Tacloban and sent three men to the post office to check on our mail, as we had not received any for two months. The three men had to come back for assistance, for they had found ten bags of mail awaiting us. What a feast our eyes had, devouring the many letters, magazines, and boxes sent from home. But along with the good word came the bad word from the base. Our stay was to be very short. We were temporarily assigned to a new flotilla, Eight, by name. We were to proceed almost immediately to Subic Bay, which is located on the island of Luzon, just above Manila Bay.

With the two days' rest, we traveled with a newly formed convoy along with the 224 toward Subic. The convoy was almost entirely composed of merchant ships, and we had quite a time interpreting their signals as they were extremely different from our landing craft signals. The trip was made in delightfully calm waters and cooling winds. Again, we made our way through the Suragao Straits, turning at Panay and passing Mindoro and the Verde Island passage separating Mindoro from Luzon. Here, most of the ships were destined for the newly freed port of Manila, and the rest of us made our way toward Subic Bay, which was to become a large amphibious base. We met a friendly submarine on the way into the bay and gave him first priority in passing through the nets enclosing the inner harbor.

Subic was not very large, but large enough to house a good sized task force and was nicely located with the natural fortifications of hills surrounding it on three sides. We met the 338 in Subic, as she was there for repairs. They had been given a rough reception on the invasion of Corregidor a week earlier. She had five 3-inch shells in her, and all but one engine knocked out. Two men had been killed, and two were wounded.

We took over some mail for her Commanding Officer, Goodman, including his stateside orders. This had given us all encouragement, for we felt that our superiors had not forgotten us. I was beginning to be enthused, for I was already on my thirteenth month and eighteen was supposed to be par for the course. There were a few omissions, such as Goodman's, who was now serving his twenty-seventh consecutive month overseas. After a friendly visit with our old pals, we retired to our anchorage on the other side of the bay.

Incoming ships are given anchorage stations by the beach master who meets the ships in a small boat and distributes charts of the bay. The areas on the charts are numbered and catalogued as to types of ships and anchorage space, for each ship is circled on the chart. We are then assigned a number, thus giving the beach master our location in case he must locate us in a hurry.

We reached our anchorage and retired for the night. The next few days brought relief for our Skipper, Jim Hofmann. In one batch of mail, he surprisingly received his orders and began preparations to turn over the ship to Don. I was to become "Exec," and Charlie was to be the new Engineering Officer. However, I was elected to retain that job, and Charlie was assigned the Gunnery Department. Jim left on the 19th of March, and we settled down in our new tasks.

Meanwhile, we had found out that we were to be on another invasion, and we had to sail to Lingayen Gulf to meet our task force. This invasion was to be on the island of Panay, which we had bypassed so often. We left on the next day for Lingayen Gulf, and we encountered very rough seas, but the trip was thankfully short, and we pulled into Lingayen with a small convoy that also had the company of the 224. We reported to the SOPA (Senior Officer Present Afloat) and retired to our assigned anchorage.

The task force was quite large, although no large ships were needed. The convoy got underway the next day, and we retraced our steps, passing Subic, Mindoro, and down to the tip of Panay, touching a bit of the straits before we turned to port and made our way into the huge gulf. On this operation, we had been assigned to a new duty. We were to assist the minesweepers.

The bay, which was very deep, even up to the beach, was also very wide and overlapped Guimaras Straits that was located below the island of Guimaras, to the east of Panay. We sailed into the bay, as usual, at dawn and took our place on the line of departure and awaited developments. This operation called for very few small boats because most of the LSTs were to edge up to the beach after the bombardment. I stood poised on the conn with my hands on the rocket switches. This was my first attempt at firing. But after the destroyers had thrown a few rounds into the beach, it was decided that no rocket bombardment would be needed, and it was called off. I was deeply disappointed.

While the LSTs and LSMs were discharging their troops on the shore, we made our way to the vicinity of the minesweepers to explode any mine with our gunfire that they "dug" up. There were five minesweepers. Our job was to follow five hundred yards behind them. No mines were found the first day, although it was rather hard on the nerves. At eighteen hundred hours, we left the "sweeps" and joined the main force that was leaving the bay. This night cruise was due to the fact that the bay was so deep, that very few ships had the scope (length) of anchor chain to reach the bottom. This cruise almost proved disastrous. The weather turned foul, and it rained continuously. The swells were high. The cruise merely took us out for four hours and then turned around and came back. But we went out too far. When we turned around to return, we had to buck the huge swells, and we pitched with alarm. Our speed was increased to nine knots. That made it worse. We couldn't see the ships ahead or astern of us, and it was dark. We were afraid of a collision. Our mast, weakened through rotting, swayed with each battering by the sea. Spray hit us in the face. We gave the ship all the speed she could maintain to keep up with the convoy. It was an unusual sight in the morning to see the large convoy scattered all over the bay.

Again, we joined the minesweepers to clean the area off Negros Island, which was adjacent to Panay and Guimaras. It was while we were on this trip that a PBM (Navy sea-plane) flew over us in distress. It was making a forced landing. The plane came to rest on the water, and one of the minesweepers and ourselves went to its rescue. It was risky business for we had to proceed through the area that we were to sweep the next day. All eyes were glued to the sea. However, we made it and pulled near the floating plane. All of the occupants were O.K., and we prepared to take her in tow. We had difficulty in securing the lines as two of them broke in the swells of the strait. But one of our boatswain mates swam to the plane with the line in his mouth and gave it to the men there. After a two-hour struggle, we got underway to return to Panay. We made it in an hour and drew in toward the beach as close as possible and anchored. The crew of the plane was brought aboard and fed and bunked for the night. The plane was finally stripped of all parts in the following days, and after making a short haul for ourselves, we took it out in the bay and sank her with 40 mm fire. The plane had one crippled engine, and it was old and decidedly useless.

On one of the subsequent days, some of the crew went ashore in the two rubber life rafts that we had procured from the plane. I went along for curiosity's sake. There was a small native village on the beach and an Army camp spread all over the premises. The natives were dirty and sloppy, evident from the small market they had, which was unsanitary to say the least. Fish and meat were on a board covered with flies and tropical insects. These were purchased and cooked to be eaten by the native population. Up the road, about ten miles, was a small modern city by the name of Iloilo (E-low, E-low). We didn't have time to explore it at this time but heard that it was a very nice place, although the Japs had raised havoc in it, and the Filipino guerillas had sacked the town.

We returned to the ship and stayed at anchor for the next few days to learn that the island of Negros was to be invaded on the 29th of March. This was just a few short hours from Panay, and very little opposition was to be expected. On the evening of the 28th, the small force slowly made its way out of the bay. This was an unusual convoy. We were part of the screen. The convoy consisted of a large group of LCVPs loaded with troops, with the second and third waves in a few LCIs. All troops had to go ashore near a long pier, which would have been very easy to defend, if any force, whatsoever, had been stationed there. We were to invade the small city of Pulupandan.

Here we were to receive our first good liberty since Tacloban.

Chapter Sixteen

WAR RELIEF

A pre-invasion bombardment was not needed as our four-knot, all-night trip brought us to the island of Negros. The troops stormed ashore on the pier and the small space on the beach next to it. The operation had no opposition whatsoever. We learned later that there were eleven Japs in the port of Pulupandan. The main force was near the city of Bacilod, fifty miles away.

We had two liberty parties the next day, one in the morning and one in the afternoon. I went ashore in the afternoon to see our newly conquered city. It was small but well organized. Immediately behind the beach was the residential section, which was one- or two-room wooden shacks on stilts. They were in a line along both sides of a dirt road. There were three such streets, one behind the other. They all converged on the city park, which at this time housed a Red Cross and medical unit for wounded soldiers. There were four cement sidewalks that led to a little bandstand that stood in the center of the park. There were small flower gardens, systematically spaced in corners around the park. The entire park was enclosed with a large iron fence.

The business section was located on the opposite side of the street that surrounded the park on three sides. To the immediate right stood the City Hall that housed the Post Office. It was empty. The building was constructed of white stucco, encircled by a huge and old iron fence. Upon entering one of two approaches, which were bordered by flower gardens, the setting was one of Spanish reflection. The keeper's tiny house and family were on the right, and they greeted all comers with politeness. Inside the building was a confusion of organization. It had all the facilities of a small town City Hall, even equipped with a large Mayor's office. Next to the City Hall was a Catholic Church.

The entire population was Catholic. The church was somewhat bare and the tiny altar all but stripped. The room was empty. A small, desolate crucifix hung over the entrance. The plaques, illustrating the Stations of the Cross were cracked, chipped, or broken. There was no Communion rail. There was no sacristy. The altar took up the tiny indentation in the front of the room. A dirty white cloth covered it and looked as if it had not been removed for years. Two statues, one of the Virgin Mary and the other of Saint Joseph, stood alone on two stands on each side of the church. A kneeling bench was the only furniture in the room. I paused and prayed, for attending church came but a few times in the Pacific. The last time had been aboard a cruiser on Christmas. Penitently, I left to look over the rest of the city. There was a Shell gasoline station, a market, an insufficient shoe store, a garage, and a restaurant, all located in frame buildings that appeared ancient.

On leaving, I was intercepted by one of the crew who told me that a guerilla chief was living in a large stucco house near the beach and gave one an interesting conversation. I immediately made my way to find an old man in army clothes and perceived that he was a Captain in the Philippine Army. He was quite difficult to understand but, during tea, he gave me a rambling description of the battle for the island. According to his testimony, he was the soother of the Japs, although I wondered at his statement, for he was outstandingly egotistical. He was the "mayor" of the town. He had been to the United States and had once applied for a commission in the Army but had been refused because of an insanity taint. He was actually warded for it. Here I left.

The natives of Pulupandan were very friendly, and I encountered many a fourteen-year-old boy who pleaded with me to take him with me to the ship. I had difficulty in refusing for they were really in earnest. Young tots, barely old enough to talk, begged for cigarettes. I took a picture of Bob, our Stewart's Mate, on a caribou. But finally, the day ended, and we made our way back to the boat to go back to the ship. Some of the crew members were late and restricted for a month. But after standing ten days' picket duty guarding the harbor, we changed the ruling. The entire convoy moved out on us, and we were left with a gunboat to challenge all comers.

However, after the ten days of doing nothing, we were relieved and proceeded to Iloilo. The change was immediate. Iloilo was a growing, modern city, and a narrow canal led into the heart of the town that housed only amphibious craft, for it was only fifty feet wide. We proceeded up the canal and docked alongside the city's railroad yards. Everyone got off the ship at the same time just to feel the ground. We were to stay there for some time. Flotilla Eight was also in the city, and Commander Martin took care of us in very good fashion. We were paid and received an enormous supply of food and beer. Liberty parties were formed, and all investigated the community. It was a very modern city, with a huge City Hall and many large and splendid homes. These belonged to the Spanish people. However, most of them had been razed by the native guerillas, for which the population was up in arms. A large park with its founder on a weather-stained statue in its center was surrounded on all sides by flower gardens. There was a large Catholic Church across from the park. On the other side was the business area that had restaurants, laundries, and all the other familiar stores of home. To us, it was the U.S.A. abroad.

We stayed in Iloilo for two weeks, but our delightful "vacation" terminated with another operation in the offing. Our fresh fruit and watermelons were soon memories. The 224 and ourselves were to proceed to Subic Bay, reporting there for another Op-Plan. We could not begin to imagine where this one was going to take us. Our guesses were the northern tip of Luzon or the rest of the Visayan group of islands that lay directly south of us. So with the 224 in the guide position, we sailed for Subic Bay. We arrived there to find that we were to invade Manila Bay, which had already been captured.

Chapter Seventeen

THE RE-INVASION OF MANILA BAY

The Skipper of the ship left with the Captain of the 224, Lt. Talberg, to visit the cruiser Phoenix to see her Captain, who was in charge of the coming operation. It was amusing information that was returned to the ship. All hands were getting somewhat tired of roaming the Philippine seas, tossing rockets on many hostile beaches and had not, as yet, forgotten their liberty at Iloilo. But here was an operation of interest to everyone. We were to invade Manila Bay and free an island called Carabao of three hundred fifty Japs. The Air Corps claimed that some anti-aircraft batteries were bothering American planes flying over the harbor and discovered that the firing was coming from this island. The operation was planned for April 16th. It was so small that no Op-Plan was delivered, but the plans were declared orally by the Captain of the Phoenix. The task force was to include two rocket ships, the 224 and the 331; two destroyers, the Nicholas and the famous O'Bannon; one cruiser, the Phoenix. That was all. Fifteen hundred troops were to make the invasion. The plan was already in effect. B-24s bombed the island three days before D-Day. Artillery on the shore near the island was peppering Carabao day and night. We were to climax the action on the 16th.

On the evening of the 15th, we sailed out of Subic Bay and traveled the 40 miles south to Manila Bay. We could hardly see our objective, the bay was so wide. But we turned in the other direction and entered Mariveles Harbor, the last stand of the men on Bataan, three years before. We dropped anchor after scouting the entire bay for the best spot. We learned the next day that the harbor was still mined. Dawn of the 16th found us steaming toward Carabao across the mouth of Manila Bay. There we met the rest of the "invasion force."

We could see the small boats filled with troops on the opposite shore. Artillery was already hammering away at the island. This island was three hundred yards along and one hundred yards wide, but it was sheer rock. There was only one spot that the forces could penetrate, and that was over a twenty-foot wall that the Phoenix had the task of knocking down. The rest of the island was protected by cliffs that rose to a height of fifty feet. The destroyers separated, and the O'Bannon took its position at the western end of the island, while the Nicholas guarded the eastern end, near our position. The 224 was over near the shore along with the troops, and the Phoenix was stationed behind and between the two rocket ships. As far as we were concerned, this was a tricky way to fire our rockets because we had to stand dead in the water, for any forward movement, and our rockets would go over the island. The current in the bay was terrific, and Don had a tough time keeping the ship steadied. Our line of departure, in other words, was twelve hundred yards or our range of rockets.

The time arrived to fire, and this was my first attempt in firing the rockets. The others had been "dry-runs." Immediately preceding our firing, we witnessed the dive-bombing tactics of eight P-51s, who strafed and bombed the objective. Then the Phoenix unloaded and sent in one round that took the wall down and engulfed the island in smoke. The destroyers began to "pop" away. We fired. The small boats began to creep closer to the objective. We could discharge only five rounds of rockets, due to the fact that we were afraid of hitting the advancing troops and also the O'Bannon sitting on the other side of the island. The troops poured ashore. It was a major operation in miniature. Our task completed, the 224 and ourselves got underway for Subic Bay. The total casualties for this operation was one Army man wounded.

We returned to Subic Bay to find that we were going to visit Leyte again. We were to leave in three days. Meanwhile, Don and I visited the city of Manila, traveling from Subic Bay on a PT boat. What a difference is forty knots on a PT boat compared to the usual maximum of ten knots on an LCI. The city of Manila was torn to shreds. There were very few buildings that were untouched by bombs or shrapnel. One could readily see that in peacetime, Manila was a beautiful modern city. We spent four hours walking the rubbled streets. We visited the Red Cross, Wilson Building, Eastern Hotel, Intramuros (the walled city), LaSalle College (Manila's home for the WACs), Nichols Airport, and the Stadium. It was our first experience in witnessing wholesale destruction.

In a short time, the 224 and ourselves again sailed through the inner sea to San Juanico Straits in northern Leyte. We arrived in Leyte on the 22nd of April and anchored near the U.S.S. Allen, which was one of the Seventh Amphibious Force's flagships. Instructions received from them gave us two new officers to be picked up from another LCI in the vicinity and a trip to Hollandia. We immediately went to the housing LCI to pick up our new officers. They proved to be Walt Street from Richmond, Virginia and George Haines from Washington, D.C. They were both ROTC graduates. This gave Don a big kick for he knew his orders were in the mail. It gave me a big jolt, too. I was to be the next Skipper! We waited for a few days until we received word that a convoy was to proceed to Hollandia, along with the 224, to undergo repairs. This would take at least a month, and all of us were glad to get away from the fighting and a hopeful rest.

The convoy was slow. It took us seven days to reach Hollandia. We had to abide by the merchant marine signals again, which proved to be a headache. But after seven days and hoping for orders for many of the crew, we arrived in Hollandia and reported to the SOPA, Commander Gardner. A new ship was in the making. A new Skipper was to take over the ship.

It was a period of excitement, of hope, disappointment, and determination.

My Log

April 14, 1945

Dearest Mother and Dad:
Pardon the laxity in writing for the past few days, but I have been answering the rest of my correspondence.

Today I will tell you about the thrill of a lifetime and to attempt to put some suspense in story form, I will begin, oddly enough, at the beginning.

Don's college roommate is a skipper on a PT boat. Don arranged to have him take us for a bit of a ride. Two officers from LCI 224 and Don and myself elected ourselves and were picked up this morning by the PT (Bob Browning). I was never so thrilled at speed over water as I was today. 35 to 40 m/h we traveled and the sea was flashing beneath us. It seemed incredible and it was certainly wonderful. After an hour or so we "flashed" around the corner of an island. There, suddenly, before us was "The Rock," otherwise known as Corregidor. What a bleak and silent monument she is. Yes, you guessed it. We continued on into Manila, 18 miles from Corregidor. When MacArthur claimed he sunk Jap ships here, he wasn't kidding. Mast after mast rose out of the water and with its yardarm created ghostly crosses. But into the city. We saw large and modern and seemingly beautiful buildings as we approached the dock. We were amazed at the city's mammoth size. It is immense. We landed and caught a ride toward town and dropped off after passing through strange odors that mark the slums. Dad, if you know anyone from Manila in the states, tell him that though the city is scarred, mangled, and hurt, it is again alive. I saw the "Great Eastern Hotel," the "Wilson Building," "The Intramuros," "La Salle College," Wilson Airfield, Dewey Boulevard, modern untouched stucco Spanish type homes, street cars (not yet running), and score upon score of automobiles: Packards, Cadillacs, Oldsmobiles, LaSalles, Lincolns, Fords, and Model A's, LaSalle Stadium, "Union Station," (trains waiting for steam), Red Cross building and scores upon scores of others. Sadly, however, I must say that the city was terrifically pounded by shell after shell, bomb after bomb.

The city is a badly mangled body with a dejected spirit, but it has a soul. It is an oasis of America here in the Orient. Prices are exorbitant. I wanted to buy a souvenir for you and Peg but I couldn't afford it. We bought one dipper of bad tasting coconut ice cream at *one small restaurant and it cost us 75 cents a piece. Cameras, like mine sell for $150.00. And do I wish I had had some film here. There are some American women, caught here by the war, WACS, Spanish girls whose prettiness dazzled me, and very pretty Filipino women. The younger men are snappy dressers and like to imitate Americans. I imagine Manila during the siege was an inferno of horrible death. The happiest moment of the day for me was when I touched my cap and smiled to a small, quite pretty, Filipino nun who returned my smile with murmuring, happy lips. She looked as if she wanted to embrace the whole U.S. Army.*

So I have seen Manila possibly for the first and last time. It lasted only four hours. I would like to return in five years and you would enjoy it also. I could have sent you a cablegram, but I entirely forgot. I'm awfully sorry for I really had it as a must.

We are finally living again. Fresh meat, potatoes, cabbage, carrots, dry provisions, beer, music, movies, and just spiced by a little work. I have so much to tell you and I'll be home so soon.

We are going to the rear lines for repairs. We will be out of the war for quite a while and having ourselves a good time. Remember the clipping on amphib recreation bases you sent me Dad?

A wonderful day is ending. I will come again.
Love, Eddie

Chapter Eighteen

REPAIRS

We arrived at Hollandia on the 4th of May. I was beginning my fifteenth month of overseas duty. On the 5th, we proceeded to the Repair Base and pulled up alongside the dock. Our work chits were ready and many in number, for we had compiled them in triplicate on the journey down. We wanted eight new engines, a new mast, new guns and gun tube, new rocket launchers, in fact, a new ship. A reception committee of five shore base officers came aboard to discover what we needed and to see how much they could help us. We were offered radar equipment, and we accepted.

With the work chits handed in for action, we began to remake the Plan of the Day accordingly and began, for the next two days, to investigate the island. We found a movie on the hill overlooking the base and an officer's club farther up the road in the interior. The base was covered with Quonset huts that housed machinery, rigging, electrical work, ordnance, and other shops. It was a complete set-up. The only flaw was that the Gunnery Officer, who had installed our rocket launchers, was now stationed at this base and no one could get along with him. However, the base was nicely organized and under a good Commanding Officer, so there was not too much to fear from being hindered. Little did I realize the sly tongue that this Gunnery Officer wagged.

The 224 was tied up on the other side of the dock, and there were four or five more ships tied up along the pier being repaired. Work commenced immediately as men from the base swarmed aboard. The deck plate above the engine room was unbolted to allow passage for the engines to be removed. The generators would also be replaced. The old rocket launchers were cut off. We were soon without electrical power and had to rely on the base to furnish the current to carry on the routine life aboard ship.

Meanwhile, Charlie and I began to frequent the club that was opened from 1600 to 1830 hours. Then we would attend the show that would begin at 1900. We would return to the ship around 2130 and have a cup of coffee and go over the day's business with Don, Walt, and George before retiring. Don was too excited to go anywhere but grabbed every mail delivery that came aboard.

The new mast was installed, and the radar technicians began to survey the job. It took them two weeks to finish it, but it was so very valuable. In the meantime, we were having trouble with the launcher situation. The new ones had not arrived, and the old ones were being repaired. But we were going to have them raised ten inches off the deck to protect the deck from the scorching it had received from the previous blasts. Repairs were going along smoothly, although new engines were not available, and we had to be satisfied with having the old ones overhauled.

On June 1st, Don received his orders, and I took over the ship. Don couldn't arrange transportation stateside for a few days and now joined us on our afternoon treks to the officer's club. He was a happy man. His term had lasted for twenty-three months.

My taking over the ship in the middle of repairs proved to be a large undertaking for me. Ten new men reported aboard, and with a complement of forty-four men, we had difficulty in bunking them all. We lost three "old timers," and they were the first to leave in many months. The repair work had already gone on for three weeks, and we were scheduled for three more. The ship was beginning to look like a new one.

One of the officers on the 224 was sent to Manus to see if he could dig up any spare parts in the area that would help us out during the repair period. He learned of the fact that new rocket launchers were on the way to us and would be delivered within two weeks. This, again, put us and the repair base in new and excellent spirits. This did not last long.

In the first week of June, we received a dispatch from the Allen that we were to be ready for an invasion by the 14th of the month, and still the launchers had not arrived. Frantically, the base renewed work on the old ones and began cutting holes in the deck for the newly planned wiring. But on the 10th of June, the launchers arrived and were immediately assembled and made ready for the installation that should have taken a week in itself. The plan of raising them off the deck was argued for a full afternoon, with the 331 coming out on top in its demand for the new idea. Thirty electricians from the base came aboard to work, day and night, on the wiring of the launchers. The holes were cut and the pipes that would house the wiring were made. The operation was completed in two days with some minor adjustments, including the wiring of five launchers by color-blind electricians. Each wire in the launcher was a different color, and the five had to be redone. I had a run-in with the Gunnery Officer, who told me that he was supervising the job, and he could do without my close "scrutiny." The argument that followed found its way to the base commander, who smoothed things out.

After the launchers were finished and ship work was finished, we were taken to a nearby dry-dock to be worked on. Two LCVPs were used to get us inside the lowered dock as our engines had not been synchronized. Pilings and lines held us fast, and the dock was raised. All hands turned to on painting the bottom with chromate, after scraping all the barnacles off. We only had twenty-four hours to complete this duty and, upon its termination, we were taken back to our repair dock.

The same evening, we left the dock under the power of two LCVPs that would take us to another dock nearby for our standing trial run. The engines were run all night and adjusted. In the morning, we were to have our regular trial run, but we had trouble with one engine and could not make it.

Meanwhile, I introduced myself to Commander Van Zandt, who was in charge of LST Group 19. We were to proceed with him to Morotai Island on the afternoon of the 13th. We were to sail with two LSTs. They had to tow three LCMs each, which was a tough job in the open seas. Without a trial run, we left the dock and proceeded to a fuel ship to take on a capacity amount. We then went out into the bay and anchored for the night.

The next morning, we got underway with the two LSTs in the lead, side by side, as we brought up the rear. The second day out, we began to have all kinds of trouble. The LCMs began to take on water. The seas began to get heavy. A violent storm was coming. For the next forty hours, I was on the conn for thirty two, taking the ship alongside and close to the battered LCMs, each manned with three men, to give them assistance. Time after time, we were called over and finally, when the storm became too much for the small convoy, the Commander elected to put into Woendi Island for repairs.

We reported into Woendi Island on the morning of the 14th and stayed three days. We received, through the efforts of the Commander, a new motor generator, as our small one had been acting up quite a bit. Also, I was invited aboard the Commander's ship for a steak dinner, of which I readily partook. The Commander informed me that he was sending a Letter of Commendation to my superior officer, which pleased me no end.

After three enjoyable days at Woendi, incidentally, the only real tropical island that I ever saw in my duty, we got underway for Morotai again. We made it on the 16th, late, but on time for the operation. We pulled into the harbor at night amidst a thousand blinking lights on the ships in the bay. We found our way to the vicinity where Flotilla One ships were stationed and anchored. We secured for the night, to arise the next morning and be informed of our new Op-Plan.

Chapter Nineteen

BALIKPAPPEN, BORNEO

On June 17th, there was a big meeting of all the Commanding Officers in the operation. This took place aboard the U.S.S. Wasatch. The operation was read and explained to all present. Our own private flotilla meeting occurred the same day under the guidance of Commander Day, who explained our part in the program. There were to be eight rocket ships and eight gunboats included in the operation. There was only one assault beach. The invasion was at Balikpapen, Borneo Island. The date for the attack was July 1st. After two such meetings with Commander Day, we were assigned dates for repairs, supplies, water, and fuel. The gunboats, which were also assigned to the same flotilla, included four LCSs for the attack. An LCS is a gunboat built on an LCI hull.

We had by this time been permanently assigned to the new flotilla, One by name, which included the sixteen rocket ships, eight gunboats, and eight LCSs. The 230, flagship for Commander Day, the 34 and ourselves spent the next two weeks together, mainly because the 230 had a movie every night, and the three Notre Dame Skippers, Grimes of the 230, Schwartz of the 34, and the 331 had been together for almost the year and a half of sea duty that each of us had put in. The flotilla was under the leadership of Commodore Arison, who had been Executive Officer on the cruiser, San Francisco, but had been wounded and instead of returning to the States, had recovered at an overseas hospital and requested continued sea duty. His flagship was the LCI (L) 778, which was beginning to become a popular headquarters, due to the fact that the flotilla was together for the first time in months.

When we had arrived, Schwartz and I decided to take the trip by small boat to the Commodore's ship to find out if any orders had been received for anyone on the ship and, to our surprise, we found orders awaiting both of us, but had not received any signatures because our relief had not yet been designated, and we had not served our full eighteen months. We soon became friends with the Personnel Officer. However, nothing could be done until after the operation, for the Commodore wanted all the ships to be at full strength for the invasion. So, with the good news in mind that we would be relieved after the ensuing operation, we went about our duties in a more cheerful manner. We made various trips to the Officer's Club as a ceremony of relief ritual. Another moment of celebration came when I was notified of my promotion to Lt. (jg) as of June 1st.

The trip to Balikpapen would take four days, and on the morning of June 27th, we left the harbor with the convoy for the trip south and westward. We knew that for thirteen days previous, there was a minesweeping Group off the Balikpapen beach, protected by a Destroyer and Cruiser Group of fighting ships. B-24s were bombing the port daily. The trip was moderately slow, with seven large transports, two dozen LSTs, LSMs, LCIs, PT boats, a Destroyer and Cruiser screen, and two Aircraft Carriers for added protection. Halfway there, we were joined by a new force of Oilers, Tankers, and a few more Destroyers. It was quite a large operation. Borneo had been hit before, on the northwest corner, at Brunei Bay, and now we were moving in on the southeast tip.

D-Day dawned, murky and listless. At the signal "Deploy," we left the convoy and proceeded ahead to our designated line of departure. Cruisers and destroyers took up positions about two thousand yards directly astern of us. The transports, all types, anchored and discharged their cargo of humans, who were to make the attack on the island. The troops were from Australia and were given American Naval support.

This operation, as far as our flotilla was concerned, was to be different. We were to make two rocket runs on the beach. One, right after dawn, and the second on leading the troops into shore. The eight gunboats, divided into two groups, were on each flank. All sixteen ships "toed" the line, waiting for the signal from Commander Day to begin our approach. Executed, it was one of the best attacks on any beach made by our flotilla. The gunboats supported with their 3-inch crossfire. Rockets were fired at the correct interval, and all ships seemed to fire at the same time. The sixteen ships were lined up from start to finish. More than four thousand rockets were sent streaming toward the beach on this attack, and all landed on the beach. After the run was completed, the 40 mms strafed the shore while the ships turned and went back to the line of departure. The cruisers and destroyers were firing shells into the beach. B-24s loomed overhead. They dropped their explosives in the hills and hit an oil dump. The concussion was felt on our ship. The B-24s returned for a second run, and the hills were covered with detonating flashes.

Meanwhile, the first wave was creeping slowly up behind us. They were protected in the slow-moving LVPs. The second wave could be seen approaching from their respective transports, forming up as they came. H-Hour was at hand. Again, we started for the beach. This time, the run was slower. Charlie handled the rockets. He waited for the range rocket from the 230 and, seeing it land on the beach, slid the controls over to number one. Rockets began to fly. We could see a slight bit of return fire. Mortars from the beach installations were falling into the sea around us. We fired round after round. The first wave was right beside us. They were indeed impressed with our support. They cheered as they passed by into the hell they knew awaited them. After they had gone, we turned and rendezvoused with the other ships in the flotilla about fifteen hundred yards to the right of the attacked beach. All hands were on the conn, and weather deck watching the proceedings, when out of nowhere, we were fired upon. Mortar fire began to fall all around us, and in more than a hurry, we weighed anchor and steamed out of the area with the rest of the "gang." One splash had lit five yards from our anchor cable. We went out further into Makasser Straits, which was somewhat "bumpy."

After watching wave after wave hit the beach and the whining of machine guns and the ping of rifles all day long, we retired for the night. To the left of the beachhead was a small river that led to the port of Balikpapen. We were to protect its right flank approach to guard the rest of the flotilla and convoy against Q-boat attacks. The 230, 337, 34, and ourselves were given the job. We were directly off the invaded beach. We had no attacks, but one morning, a Jap plane flew over us and, in the mist, seemed to be right over our heads. That was the only "opposition" we saw. The next few days were spent in watching an artillery duel on the side of a hill to the right of the beach. The Japs were giving the "Aussies" quite a bit of trouble in the hills. Five days later, we left the area. We returned with some empty LSTs and some of our flotilla to Morotai. Immediately on landing, we were notified that we were going to Subic Bay. A new duty awaited us there. It was a month-long training period, during which time we would train various divisions for the invasion of Japan, although at the time, we did not know that that was their destination. A few of the ships left early. We followed in a small convoy with seven other ships in our flotilla, arriving at Subic where most of the entire group was now based.

Schwartz, Grimes, and I reported aboard the flagship in hopes of receiving our orders. Upon checking with the Personnel Officer, we found out that he was trying to get our orders signed by the Commodore so that we could go home. After a day of parrying, they were handed to us, signed by Arison, after his return from the Officer's Club. Joyfully, we returned to our ships, which were tied up together and began to pack, not fully realizing, as yet, what had happened. We went over to the Officer's Club to celebrate and returned to the ships for a last movie and another beer before hitting the sack for the last time aboard. It was hard to realize that my eighteen months had been climaxed so suddenly.

I was going home.

Chapter Twenty

THE LAST LAP

The ceremony involved in being relieved is very short. I gave my little speech to the crew the day before, and all I had to dc was read my orders, and the officer taking over the ship would read his orders, and the ship would be his. The entire crew was mustered for the rite. It was the morning of July 29th. I had signed all the log books I could get my hands on the previous evening. Now, with the orders as the only obstacle between me and the first leg home, I took them to the weather deck, where the crew was standing at attention, greeted my relief, Ensign Hatch, Engineering Officer of the 230 with Charlie, Walt, and George reflecting my happiness with a smile.

I read my orders, which stated that I was relieved of my present duties and would take the first available transportation to the U.S.A. Then Hatch read his orders. I shook his hand and wished him luck. I retired to my cabin to load my gear aboard the 230, where Frank and Roy were waiting for me. We then waited for a small boat and, upon obtaining one, made our way to the beach. We had planned, beforehand, that we would not try to get transportation from Subic but were going to visit Manila and leave from there. The three of us had fantastic ideas about hitting Sidney, Australia and Honolulu, Hawaii on the way home, or, at least, going through the Panama Canal. We hopped a truck for the city, forty miles away.

We arrived in Manila in the early evening and were surprised by its largeness. In my prior four-hour journey here in April, I did not think it was so expansive. We made our way to the Red Cross Building to see if we could get a room anywhere for a few nights. But there was a housing shortage. We were given the Y.M.C.A. as our only hope, so we made our way there, which was only three blocks from the Red Cross. The beds were pure boards and rated at twenty-five cents per night, but we were told of a private home that had inner spring mattresses on their beds for fifty cents per night. We accepted and walked two more blocks down into a small side street with no lights and stopped before an old frame house complete with fence. It took some time to arouse the occupants, but finally a small door opened, and a face glared out at us (just like the old speakeasy) and, seeing that we were customers, invited us in for a good night's rest. Our inner spring mattresses turned out to be more steel springs, and the mattresses were straw mats. A mosquito net protected the sleeper from malaria, but, as we found out later, there was nothing to protect us from the bedbugs.

We left the next day and turned our orders over to the proper authorities and were given waiting orders on an APL, which is a large barge converted into a hotel. We had many of the comforts of home here. In the two days at Manila, we camera'ed our way through the sights. We were notified of our assignment to a ship bound for Pearl Harbor and fount it to be an APA, the U.S.S. John Land. The day before boarding the ship, we visited Cavite, the large Naval base located near Manila that the U.S. Navy used in peacetime. The base had been blasted pretty badly. Frank, Roy, and I took a ride in a little horse and buggy affair that traveled through the small town of Cavite and, when we asked the driver that we would like to see some pretty girls, he, without hesitation, took us to the edge of town to a houseful of ladies who were engaged in the occupation of "morale building." Red-faced, we returned to the town and soon retired for the evening.

We went aboard ship on the 2nd of August and were given bunks in the hottest officer's quarters I have ever encountered. We slept on deck until we began to stand fire control watches, which meant that we were assigned to keep the ship's signalmen awake.

We were glad to see the islands of Hawaii hove into view, after sixteen tormenting days aboard that ship.

On August 14th, we heard of the Japanese capitulation. The whole ship celebrated. This meant that we might not have to return to sea duty.

Unloaded at Pearl Harbor, we were assigned to the Bachelor Officer's Quarters, along with a new friend, Lt. Fredericks of YMS duties in the Pacific. He was from Allentown, Pa. Frank left on a carrier three days later, and the rest of us were destined for nine days total in becoming used to living like human beings again.

Honolulu, Oahu, was really Paradise for it was like the States. We drank milk by the quarts, our first taste of the golden dew in almost two years. Honolulu is American in taste. Department stores, drug stores, taxis, filling station, and all that goes with everyday American life. Besides, there was the Moa Huana Hotel, Waikiki Beach, and the Royal Hawaiian Hotel, which was now being used as rehabilitation for submariners, the souvenir shops along the beach, the beautiful gardens and palm trees, and the deepest tint of green in the grass. It was like heaven on earth. We shopped at the various stores for presents for the family and friends.

Frank had received some kind of a break when he was notified early that he was to leave on one of the "baby carriers" as a passenger for the States. The three of us left waited another six days before we were assigned space aboard the U.S.S. Altamaha, an Escort Carrier.

The trip to the States lasted five days. Roy and I slept on the hanger deck, while Fredericks, being a full lieutenant, slept in the regular officer's staterooms. The chow was very good, and we enjoyed the five days immensely. On the last morning, with fog rolling and the rain threatening our arrival, we spotted the huge sign in San Francisco Bay that read, "Welcome Home. Well Done."

Then, in the swirls of fog, we distinguished the Golden Gate Bridge, a sight that some of us thought we would never see again, the last time we passed beneath her mighty spans.

The ship docked while a Navy Band played "California, Here I Come."

When detached, we made our way to the heart of the city where we found a room at the Palace Hotel. Then, phone calls and telegrams – and our families knew that we were home safely.

[There's an apocryphal story, and I am not sure of its truth, but I want it to be true, that when my father called the Vlossak home to speak to Peggy, Peggy was at the movies. Betty Vlossak, who was her older brother's wife, ran down Palmerton's Delaware Avenue, the town's main street, where the Vlossaks lived, a few blocks from the movie theater. Betty ran into the theater, past the usher, and yelled into the dark room, "Peggy! Pat's on the phone!" – Peggy jumped

up, hand on her hat, and raced up the aisle as Betty yelled, "He's back from the war!" and the audience cheered and applauded. Peggy raced down the street to the waiting phone while Betty found a seat to finish watching the movie and could report on how that, too, ended happily. And now, back to my father's report.]

According to our orders, we had four days to ourselves. Upon turning in our orders, I made arrangements to fly home to Dayton. I called that decision home and told them that I would arrive on September 5th (my birthday) and also sent a telegram to Peg to get to Dayton as soon as possible.

At 8:30 PM, the flight took off that sent me through Los Angeles, Albuquerque, Phoenix, Wichita, Kansas City, St. Louis, Indianapolis, and at last, to Dayton. It was my first plane ride and I was scared [Note that in those days, the plane would have stopped at each of those cities]. An Air Force Colonel, stationed at Wright-Paterson Field, sat beside me, and finding out that it was my first trip up, commented on all the things he said were wrong with the flight. The trip had taken over nineteen hours from the West Coast. As the plane landed at the Dayton airport, I stepped to the door of the plane to see my mother and dad waiting for me at the gate.

It was true. I was home.

I was met by Peg three hours later as she had flown for the first time from Allentown to Toledo to Dayton and everyone had a happy reunion that was slated to last for thirty-four days. There was also our planned marriage of which the date was now set for the 18th of September.

After greetings to family and friends alike, Peg and I left for her home to make last minute arrangements for our wedding. Five days were spent at her home, with our folks and a few relatives driving up for the big occasion.

The wedding was held on the 18th in a little town outside of Palmerton, called Bowmanstown, and we left for our honeymoon in the Pocono Mountains, equipped with four bottles of Scotch and four of Champagne. But on the 20th, we received quite a jolt when we were telephoned from home that my leave was cancelled and that I was to report to Great Lakes on the 22nd for the Demobilization

School there. We drove to Dayton, where we stayed overnight, and then continued to Chicago, where I reported in for the new school. After two weeks of training, I was assigned to Boston's Separation Center and we made our trip via Dayton and Palmerton in our allotted five days.

Arriving in Boston found us facing the acute housing shortage, but luck was with us, and we found a five-room furnished apartment in the suburb of Newtonville. Then we looked forward to my discharge on June 1st.

My duties in the Center were merely that of Division Officer along with Lt. Radvilas, Lt (jg)'s Urquhart, MacDonald, Tice, and Lovell. It was the method assigned me by the Bureau of Personnel to pass the time until I caught up with the point system. My Navy life was almost over.

The Navy had taught me with more serious determination to know how to take care of myself and, through discipline, accept responsibility. It had given me the foundation of life I had been seeking for so long. I believed that I was ready to accept any challenge that life held for me.

THE SECRETARY OF THE NAVY

WASHINGTON

August 6, 1946
My dear Lieutenant (jg) Sheeran:

I have addressed this letter to reach you after all the formalities of your separation from active service are completed. I have done so because, without formality but as clearly as I know how to say it, I want the Navy's pride in you, which it is my privilege to express, to reach into your civil life and to remain with you always.

You have served in the greatest Navy in the world.

It crushed two enemy fleets at once, receiving their surrenders only four months apart.

It brought our land-based airpower within bombing range of the enemy, and set our ground armies on the beachheads of final victory.

It performed the multitude of tasks necessary to support these military operations.

No other Navy at any time has done so much. For your part in these achievements, you deserve to be proud as long as you live. The Nation which you served at a time of crisis will remember you with gratitude.

The best wishes of the Navy go with you into your future life. Good luck!

Sincerely yours,
James Forrestal

APPENDIX

The following news articles are from Dayton, Ohio newspapers during the war. I believe they are primarily from the *Dayton Journal*. My grandfather, Edward Patrick Sheeran, kept a map in his living room and, based on a code he and my father used (and I assume my uncle, Don, who was in France), my grandfather would mark the spots where his sons were. He also collected newspaper articles concerning the fighting arenas where sons Ed and Don were. Here are a few. Unfortunately, the dates of the articles were not included. The styling of spelling and punctuation have been retained.

SANTA DELIVERS 2,200 BAGS OF GIFTS TO LEYTE
LEYTE ISLAND, P.I., Dec. 2 [Saturday] – Approximately 2,200 bags of Christmas parcels have arrived for Yanks on Leyte.
Maj. J.B. De Mott, Boston, Mass., army postal inspector, said 506 bags had been delivered to the 1st cavalry division after being forwarded from the Admiralties. An additional 1,700 bags for other units have arrived from New Guinea and are awaiting distribution. Maj. De Mott said none of the parcels had been damaged in transit.
G.I.'s here still are wishing for envelopes that won't seal themselves automatically in the Philippines humidity, but Maj. De Mott and the post office department have given up the search for a suitable glue. He said thousands of mothers had protested over mutilated envelopes in the belief mail from their sons had been opened by persons other than censors.

EVENTS IN PHILIPPINE WAR

ASSOCIATED PRESS

Highlights of the war in the Philippines:

Manila first bombed by the Japanese December 8, 1941.

Japanese landed in Philippines December 10, 1941.

Japanese took Manila January 2, 1942.

Gen. Douglas MacArthur, ordered out of Philippines, arrived in Australia March 17, 1942, saying "I will return."

Bataan surrendered April 9, 1942.

Corregidor fell May 6, 1942.

Japanese Navy sustained heavy losses June 18-19, 1944 in first battle of Philippine Sea, fought between air and surface forces at the time of the American invasion of the Marines.

MacArthur's communique of July 24, 1944 made first mention of Philippines, reporting raids on enemy shipping off Mindanao.

First raids on the Philippines, staged from Southwest Pacific August 6-8, 1944 since the April 15, 1942 attack from Corregidor on Clark Field.

First heavy bomber struck against Philippines, September 3, 1944.

First American carrier aircraft attack on archipelago made Vice Adm. William F. Hasey's Task Force September 8, 1944. Other carrier attacks quickly followed.

First carrier plane smashed at Manila September 21, 1941.

On September 24, 1944, Adm. Chester W. Nimitz said carrier operations had forced "the enemy to withdraw his naval forces from their former anchorage in the Philippines and to seek new refugees in the same general area."

American amphibious forces land October 20, 1944 on Leyte Island, in first reinvasion of the archipelago.

Japanese Navy met its second great disaster in Philippine waters October 21-26, 1944, losing many warships in costly attempt to interfere with the invasion of Leyte.

Americans land on Mindoro Island, December 15, 1944, broadcast an editorial warning that the victor on Mindoro "will assume full control of tomorrow's military situation."

Marinduque Island, just east of Mindoro and south of Luzon, invaded by Americans from Mindoro on January 6.

THREE JAP SHIPS SUNK BY 2 SUBS
FREDERICK C. SHERMAN, ADMIRAL U.S. NAVY, RETIRED
In preparation for the landing at Leyte gulf a large group of our submarines had been stationed in the areas between the Philippines and Singapore to give warning of the approach of Japanese forces from that direction. In the early morning hours of Oct. 22, 1944, the submarines Darier and Dace, on the alert off Palawan, made the first contacts in the second battle of the Philippines sea.

These submersibles made out what they thought were three cruisers in the darkness, but lost contact and found nothing during daylight of that day. The next night, again shortly after midnight, another contact was made with a much larger force.

This time it was the main fleet from Singapore and consisted of five battleships, 12 cruisers and 15 destroyers. It was what later became known as the central force and was proceeding up Palawan passage bound for Leyte gulf via the Sibuyan sea and San Bernardino strait. The rest of Admiral Kurita's ships had been left under Admiral Nishimura at Brunei bay in Borneo to proceed independently to Leyte gulf via the Sulu sea and Surigao strait.

Nishimura's division slipped into the Sulu sea between Borneo and Palawan while our submarines were preoccupied with Kurita's fleet and was undetected until slighted by planes from the Enterprise of task force 38 on the morning of the twenty-fourth. It contained two 30,000 ton battleships, Fuso and Yamashiro, the heavy cruiser Mogami and four destroyers. Although 26 Enterprise search planes joined up to attack this force only minor damage was inflicted.

Later that morning another search plane sighted Admiral Shima's fifth fleet coming down from the Pescadores and heading southeast across the Sulu sea. It was assumed by our high command to be the same force sighted earlier because it was composed of two heavy cruisers, one light cruisers and four destroyers, the same number of ships as previously reported. It was not attacked prior to its entry into Surigao strait that night, nor was Nishimura's after the ineffective attack of the Enterprise search planes.

Admiral Kinkaid was unaware that two separate forces were approaching to enter the southern gateway to the gulf and thought he had to deal with only one. Admiral Halsey was concentrating his entire effort on Kurita's central force father north.

This set the stage for the surface engagement in Surigao strait and enabled the battleships to participate in the destruction of that part of the Japanese navy.

There is little doubt that, if sufficient air effort had been diverted against these Jap groups, they would never have reached the strait. However, Admiral Kinkaid considered he had plenty of strength to take care of them without calling on the aviators.

Our two submarines in contact with Kurita's force shortly after midnight on the twenty-third decided their scouting roles was more important than a night attack and waited until daylight for identification of the types encountered. Using their radars, they took position ahead of the two enemy columns and proceeded along with them like two unseen pilot vessels leading the way. They sent off three contact reports in the night and estimated the force to consist of 11 heavy ships.

At dawn the submarines submerged and took positions for a co-ordinated attack. The Darter, under command of Commander David H. McClintock, struck first, taking the port column.

Ten torpedoes were fired at the leading ship and five explosions were counted. Swinging hard eft to fire the stern tubes at the second ship, four hits were estimated on this target. Then the Darter quickly went down deep to avoid depth charges and was unable to see the final results.

The Dace, under command of Commander B.D. Claggett, saw two cruisers burning as a result of the Darter attack and picked the third ship in the starboard column as her target.

Firing six torpedoes, she obtained four hits before forced to deep submergence by enemy destroyers. Amid the thunder of many depth charges both submarines got away unharmed.

Through evidence obtained after the war it was established that the heavy cruiser Atago suffered four hits from the Darter and sank; the heavy cruiser Takao took two hits from the same source and had to be abandoned, while the heavy cruiser Maya got four hits from the Dace and sank. Thus crippled from the loss of three important ships and shaken in morale, Kuria's force continued toward its rendezvous with destiny in Leyte gulf.

JAPS IN ISLANDS ARE SPLIT BY MACARTHUR
FORCE LANDING ON LEYTE
FOE CAUGHT UNAWARES
GENERAL FULFILLS HIS PLEDGE TO RETURN—
SHOWDOWN BATTLES AT HAND
ASSOCIATED PRESS,
ARMY RADIO POOL BROADCAST
GENERAL MACARTHUR'S HEADQUARTERS IN THE PHILIPPINES, Oct. 20 (Friday) – (AP) – Gen. Douglas MacArthur, making good his vow he would return to the Philippines, announced from those islands today his Navy and air supported forces have invaded and secured expanding beachheads in the Central Philippines.

"In a major amphibious operation we have seized the eastern coast of Leyte Island in the Philippines, 600 miles north of Morotai and 2,500 miles from Milne Bay (New Guinea)" a special communique dramatically proclaimed from the invasion scene.

Striking at a point where he is in position to quickly cut off the Island of Luzon, on which Manila is situated from Mindanao on the south, MacArthur poured supplies down battles with an estimated 225,000Japanese under Filed Marshal Juichi Terauch.

PRESIDENT IS STIRRED
The greatest moment to date in the Pacific war brought immediate acclamation of MacArthur's invasion forces by President Roosevelt in Washington.

"The whole American nation today exalts at the news that the gallant men under your command have landed on Philippine soil," the President said.

On Leyte, a suitable air base island 300 miles southeast of Manila, the invaders secured Tacloban on the northeast end of the island "with small casualties," the communique reported.

Tokyo radio also reported landings at Cabalian on the southern tip and said earlier landings occurred at the entrance of Leyte Gulf on Suluan Island.

[part of article missing]

Tokyo said that in addition to the Manila area, 420 miles northwest of the Leyte Gulf area, 425 miles northwest of the Leyte Gulf area, American planes attacked all the way from Aparri in Northern Luzon to Cebu and Taclebal – capital of Leyte Island—in the invasion zone.

An Allied fleet – presumably the Eastern Fleet under Adm. Sir Bruce Fraser – at the same time made a diversionary attack with shell and bomb on the Nicabor Islands in the Indian Ocean, Japan said.

MacArthur's planes heavily attacked Mindanao Island, south of the invasion area, and the Haahera Islands, south of the Philippines, in which MacArthur had captured Morotai Island September 14.

BOMBERS RAKE TARGETS
More than 50 heavy bombers heavy bombers, MacArthur said, raked targets around Davao and Zamboanga Tuesday. Fighters returned Wednesday to hit Cotobato, on the east-central coast of Mindanao.

[article illegible]
Fighters, hitting Cotabato Wednesday, strafed a motor convoy and small shipping.

YANKS LAND 150 MILES FROM MANILA
ASSOCIATED PRESS
C. YATES McDANIEL
MAC ARTHUR'S HEADQUARTERS, Philippines, Dec. 16 – (AP) – A naval-borne U.S. Sixth Army force crossed the Philippines and gained a virtually bloodless beached on Mindoro island, within 150 miles of Manila, Friday morning (Philippine time), Gen. Douglas MacArthur disclosed today.

The daring amphibious break spanning the heart of the Japanese-dominated Philippines established for the Americans an east-west corridor through the archipelago which will give them access to routes leading to the coast of China, the supreme commander said.

Swarms of carrier-based planes Friday and the day before scourged virtually every Nipponese airfield in the far-flung archipelago, destroying more than 200, perhaps 300, enemy aircraft.

The 600-mile overwater movement took the convoy from Leyte, where the Americans first landed Oct. 20, south and west past the Japanese-occupied islands of Mindanao, Bohol,

Cebu, Negros and Panay, but heroic guerrillas meanwhile had turned it into a fairly safe convoy by seizing airfields and strategic ports along the way in secret actions just disclosed.

Three beachheads were established quickly on southern Mindoro. Elmont Waite, Associated Press war correspondent, told of tanks rolling ashore, of bulldozers starting roads, of piers being erected and of engineers moving inland with the troops to construct vase installations.

(Tokyo radio said the landings occurred near San Jose, which is on Mindoro's southwest coast, and were made by about a division, which ordinarily would be around 15,000 men. The enemy broadcast was without allied confirmation.

LAND 130 MILES FROM MANILA WITHOUT CASUALTIES; TOKYO SAYS AIR-SEA SCRAP RAGES
UNITED PRESS

American invasion troops swarmed over Mindoro island within 130 miles of Manila today in a hazardous but strongly-supported amphibious thrust that threatened, at a single stroke, to cut the Philippines in two and sever Japan's sea communications with her southern empire.

The surprise landing was effected without a single casualty yesterday at the height of a blazing two-day aerial strike on adjoining Luzon, during which American naval and land-based planes knocked out half the Japanese air force on that island and sank or damaged every ship in Manila bay.

Veteran American assault troops, drawn from the forces now bringing the battle of Leyte into its final stages, drove swiftly inland from at least three beachheads on the southwest coast of Mindoro, striking for two of the island's eight airfields.

Japanese broadcasts said the island garrison, which apparently was caught off guard by the initial landing, was reacting strongly and that fierce fighting was in progress.

Tokyo also asserted that a violent air-sea battle was raging off Mindoro and assorted Japanese flyers sank or damaged 25 American warships and transports in a three-day attack on the invasion convoy. There was no confirmation of the enemy reports, which placed the invading force at a full division, or about 15,000 men.

YANK TROOPS DRIVE INLAND ON MINDORO
MACARTHUR WADES ASHORE ON LUZON AFTER
TORPEDOES WHIZ BY HIS SHIP
GENERAL WELL PLEASED WITH LATEST EXPLOIT
IN BELOVED ISLANDS
ASSOCIATED PRESS
GENERAL MACARTHUR'S HEADQUARTERS, PHILIPPINES, Jan. 10 (Wednesday) – (AP) – Wearing his famed campaign hat and five stars on his collar, Gen. Douglas MacArthur returned to Luzon with his assault troops Tuesday morning.

Two torpedoes from a midget submarine missed his ship as the convoy headed for the landing. MacArthur then rode upon the engine box of a landing craft and waded knee deep in water onto the soil of Luzon he left nearly three years ago. He hit the shore about two hours after the first wave.

MacArthur talked with privates and Generals alike and expressed himself pleased with the way the operation was proceeding.

In the boat which took MacArthur to Lingayen Beach were his aides, Col. Lloyd Lehrbas, Pocatello, Idaho, and Lt. Col. Roger Egberg, Cleveland, Ohio, and three of the men who accompanied the Genera in his flight from Corregidor – Lt. Gen. Richard Sutherland, Maj. Gen. Richard Marshall and Spencer Akin.

Also with the party was Warrant Officer Paul Rogers and Sgt. Adam Shorter, Altoona, Pa., the one American Marine who went ashore with MacArthur.

Shorter had stood guard outside MacArthur's cabin aboard the warship which brought him to Luzon. When he General found out that his guard had a brother in one of the army divisions taking part in the landing, he obtained permission for Shorter to make the landing in the hope of finding his brother. Earlier [unreadable] on Lingayen Gulf for several hours, talking to the troops who included Filipinos.

The landing was made in bright sunshine, with American fighter planes patrolling overhead.

A hundred yards from shore MacArthur saw the American flag waving from a [blurred] assault boat crunched onto the beach.

Just before MacArthur's boat beachhead infantrymen ashore were hunting down a Japanese sniper he added.

Touring the beachhead, MacArthur met a soldier, stripped to the waist

[rest missing]

COAST TOWNS ARE TAKEN IN JAPAN'S
STRONGHOLD OF PHILIPPINE GROUP
M'ARTHUR IN COMMAND
AMERICAN LOSSES ARE LIGHT IN TAKING
15-MILE STRIP, 107 MILES FROM MANILA

ALLIED HEADQUARTERS, LEYTE, PHILIPPINES, Jan. 10 (Wednesday) – (UPI) – Veteran U.S. Sixth Army troops invaded the main Philippines island o Luzon yesterday from an 800-ship armada, establishing a 15-mile beachhead on Lingayen Gulf against Japanese resistance so beaten down by a three-day bombardment that not one American in the first attack was reported killed.

The Americans, under the personal command of Gen. Douglas MacArthur, who went ashore with his men, quickly seized several coastal towns, among them San Fabian, on the southeastern corner of the gulf, 109 miles northwest of Manila.

A headquarters spokesman said some forces had reached points within 107 miles of Manila on the south coast.

FEW JAPS ON HAND

The Americans went ashore at 9:30 a.m., Philippine time, and encountered only a few bursts of artillery and mortar fire. Front dispatches said there were no few Japanese defending the beaches, that only a handful of enemy troops were killed.

"The Japs refused to fight," said one United Press dispatch from the front.

The Japanese had offered stubborn resistance to the preliminary three-day air and sea bombardment – one American Admiral said it was worse than at Saipan. They inflicted some losses on our ships [copy cut off] carrier planes began a three-day bombardment of Luzon. The bombardment was resumed yesterday morning at dawn, clearing the way for the veteran troops who went ashore in landing craft. It was Krueger's troops who also had invaded Leyte and Mindanao.

JAPS LOSE PLANES

The Japanese, attempting to break up the naval formations of Vice Adm. Thomas C. Kinkaid's Seventh Feet and units of Adm. William F. Halsey's famed Third Fleet, lost 79 planes, a midget submarine and two destroyers. The midget submarine attacked the formation on the way to Luzon, fired two torpedoes which missed, and was sank by a destroyer which rammed it. The destroyers were observed by warplanes and naval forces immediately raced in and sank them.

In addition, the Japanese lost one coastal cargo ship and many small harbor and coastal craft during the preinvasion air and sea bombardments.

JAPS REPORT U.S. CONVOY IN SULU SEA

UNITED PRESS

The Japanese reported that American carrier-based assault on Luzon entered its second day today and claimed also that a "powerful" Allied convoy sailed westward through the central

Philippines in what was described as foreshadowing a major operation to expand American lines in the islands.

The enemy broadcasts, recorded by FFC, came as Gen. Douglas MacArthur's forces on Leyte rushed into the final stage of a campaign that in 55 days has cost the Japanese more than 82,000 casualties.

Tokyo said the second day assault on Luzon was carried out by approximately 400 planes from a U.S. task force in the eastern Philippines waters.

A Domei dispatch said the convoy sailed westward through the Mindanao strait and into the Sulu sea and pointed out that "this enemy surface unit is nothing to make light of."

HIT MANILA AREA
The Japanese reported, according to the FFC, that 100 planes attacked Clark Field area near Manila while some 300 others were over other parts of Luzon and the Visayan area.

A United Press correspondent with the U.S. carrier force off Luzon reported that naval airmen had destroyed an estimated 147 Japanese planes in yesterday's assault on Luzon.

American Superfortresses from Saipan continued their almost daily forays against central Japan this morning. The enemy radio described the attacks as "nuisance" fire raids on Tokyo and reconnaissance fights over the arsenal cities of Kobe and Osaka.

The Kobe-Osaka district is probably the most important industrial target in Japan, and the observation flights suggested that both cities are likely soon to be visited in force by the B-29's.

Yanks May Be On Luzon, Jap Radio Asserts
NEW YORK, Jan. 6 – UP – The Tokyo radio said today "The Americans may have landed on Luzon."

This statement was regarded by London after Tokyo had reported a big American armada with landing craft and transports off Luzon, the main island of the Philippines.

Similar Japanese brodcasts (sic) were heard in the United States.

The Japanese Domei News Agency said today that "Three groups of enemy transports with carrier protection appeared in the Philippine waters Friday, apparently with the intention of attempting landings somewhere, probably at Luzon." There was no allied confirmation.

The dispatch recorded by the Federal Communications Commission said that one convoy, comprising "about 100 landing craft escorted by a task force" penetrated waters west of Lingayen bay, Luzon.

Another "large group of United States vessels," said Domei, "together with about

10 converted aircraft carriers" was reported cruising west of Panay Island.

The third convoy reported by Domei was "sighted speeding westward in waters south of Negros Island."

In a broadcast beamed to China, radio Tokyo said that "The battle for the Philippines will decide the outcome of the greater East Asia war." It added that "The Leyte and Mindoro campaigns are merely local operations" and the "decisive struggle" will take place on Luzon.

Luzon is the main island of the Philippines. Manila is located on it.

EDWARD FRANCIS "PAT" SHEERAN

(1920-1993)

Pat Sheeran was born in Van Wert, Ohio on September 5, 1920, the youngest of three children (brother Donald and sister Lillian) of Edward Patrick and Mary Elizabeth Sheeran. He graduated from the University of Dayton in April 1943. A veteran of World War II, he served in the South Pacific, primarily in the Philippines. An officer onboard the USS LCI (R) 331, and ultimately its Skipper, he fought in eleven major naval operations, including the historic battle over Leyte.

After leaving the South Pacific, Pat married Margaret Vlossak of Palmerton, Pennsylvania. Once he served out his naval assignment in Boston, he entered civilian life as a salesman with the Coca-Cola Bottling Company of Palmerton, founded by his father-in-law Frank Vlossak, a Hungarian immigrant. In 1950, Pat became Sales Manager of that company's plant in Washington, New Jersey and then full Manager from 1960 to 1970, during which time, he won several sales awards. In 1971, he and Peggy moved to Findlay, Ohio, where Pat managed a Pepsi-Cola plant for the Pepsi Beverages Company of Lima, Ohio.

In Washington, New Jersey, Pat was an officer and member of the Lions Club and a member of the Holy Name Society of Saint Joseph's Roman Catholic Church, where he coached the parish's basketball team, was a religious instructor to high school boys, and sang in the church choir (along with Peggy and daughter Mary) for several years. He also served on Washington's town council.

In Findlay, Pat served as an officer of Optimist International and was a major promoter of the ultimately successful movement to designate Findlay as Flag City, USA, which occurred on May 7, 1974 by House Joint Resolution #1003. Pat was also a member of Findlay's Chamber of Commerce from 1985 to 1987. Both Pat and Peggy were members of Sycamore Springs Golf Club. Sycamore Springs remembers Peggy (who took on golf with an award-winning vengeance after the kids left home) on its sixth hole, beneath what she called "that damn tree."

Pat and Peggy's romance never ended, despite three interruptions, namely, Michael, Patrick, and Mary. They enjoyed and supported their kids, helping them ultimately through college and into life. After Mary graduated from college, Pat and Peggy enjoyed their new independence, their golfing, and their friends, but in 1984, Peggy was diagnosed with lung cancer.

Pat cared for Peggy throughout the years of her illness. After she passed away in 1987, Pat, by then retired, moved to Arlington, Virginia where he too passed away in August 1993.

Pat and Peggy now rest together in Arlington National Cemetery.

www.ingramcontent.com/pod-product-compliance
Lightning Source LLC
Chambersburg PA
CBHW020516100426
42813CB00030B/3270/J